Heterogender Homosexuality in Honduras

Heterogender Homosexuality in Honduras

Manuel Fernández-Alemany and Stephen O. Murray

Writers Club Press
San Jose New York Lincoln Shanghai

Heterogender Homosexuality in Honduras

Writers Club Press
an imprint of iUniverse, Inc.

For information address:
iUniverse, Inc.
5220 S. 16th St., Suite 200
Lincoln, NE 68512
www.iuniverse.com

ISBN: 0-595-22681-7

Printed in the United States of America

Contents

PREFACE

This book describes and analyzes the sexual culture of same-sex (but heterogender) sex in the Honduran city of San Pedro Sula. It is based on the dissertation fieldwork and the University of Southern California dissertation of Manuel Fernández-Alemany, who was born and raised in Santiago, Chile. The book's introduction details how he came to do fieldwork in Honduras. My own fieldwork on Latin American male homosexualities was done further north—in Guatemala City, Mexico City, and East Oakland, California—and I have never officially been in Honduras. That I once physically visited Honduras but that this did not register in public records (passports, visas, etc.) seems appropriately analogous to those men who penetrate male bodies but do not regard themselves and are not regarded by others as engaging in homosexuality even (or especially) by those whose male bodies they penetrate.

The schema that only the penetrated one is "homosexual" is widespread. It was the predominant conception in the largest US city before World War II (see Chauncey 1994), continued to be widely credited in North American cities during the decades after it (see Leznoff 1954), and has not altogether disappeared even in such "gay Meccas" as San Francisco in the 21st century. (Indeed, the return of the repressed, in this instance the gender-variant "queer," and the "I have sex with males but don't want to be defined by that" attitude are flourishing in the US of the present.)

When I began visiting Mesoamerica in the mid-1970s (as I have written about in Murray 1996b), I saw signs that the heterogender homosexuality, which I thought was archaic and destined to disappear, was being challenged by the development of "modern gay" organization of homosexual relationships. In the late-1970s, I noticed that the word *gay* was diffusing, but that, instead of necessarily signifying raising the penetrated male to equality with his penetrators (stigma trans-valuation), it was, for many, simply a new label (relexification) of the old concept *pasivo, maricón*, etc. Variance in, first, familiarity with the term, and, then, in its meaning and place in organizing and valuing same-sex sexual relationship, and the differential familiarity with various other labels (specifically, a familiarity with more terms by *pasivos*) became the subject of my first publication on Latin America (Murray 1980b). Way back then, I also expressed doubts about the inevitability of "modern gay" homosexuality developing without the structural bases (such as reliable social insurance, relatively meritocratic labor markets, and housing stock available to unmarried individuals) of the development in countries of the north (Murray 1980a, expanded into Murray 1987:118-28, and revised as Murray 1995:33-48).

This book shows that the heterogender stratification into masculine-heterosexual penetrators of feminized homosexuals continues. Indeed, fueled perhaps in part by gender being the "master discourse" of turn-of-the-millennium anthropology (what I call "the Empire of Gender"—see Murray 1996:161-66), transgendered male prostitutes have been the primary focus of recent ethnographic research on Latin American homosexuality, including books by Don Kulick and Annick Prieur, and a special issue of *Sexualities* (1,3) edited by Kulick, all published in 1998; and a 1999 book by Jacobo Schifter. Male prostitutes have also been the focus of diplomatic historian Jacobo Schifter's (1998, 2000) research in Costa Rica from a perspective that seeks and finds widespread and sometimes fatal victimization as the basis for heterogender homosexual relations.

Dr. Fernández-Alemany's text explores the agency of the feminized homosexuals of lower-class San Pedro and the perspectives of their masculinist partners who stress friendship and mutual assistance rather than the domination, extortion, and violence of the *cacheros* and *chapulines* who interest (attract?) Schifter (see Fernández-Alemany 2000 on the voyeurism of Schifter's writings). We at least think that we know what thieves and bordello employees think they are doing, but what masculine young men who have penetrative sexual relationships with those defined as "homosexuals" think they are doing has been mysterious, because they have heretofore been either unwilling to speak or inarticulate (see Carrier 1995:198; Murray 1996b; Kulick 1998; Prieur 1998:179-233,). The insight into the *hombres'* definition of their situation as partners of homosexual males is what is most novel in the research reported here.

This research establishes that the penetrating roles are played by males mostly between the ages of 15 and 25, ages in which experimentation is more permissible than it will be once marriage is expected for males in their mid-20s. Those able to pay (and, in the cultural logic, **obligated** to pay) to be penetrated are older. The young *hombres* instantiate the subtype "boy top" of the "age-stratified" category within the typology of homosexualities in my 2000 book. Although the sexual partners in lower-class Honduras same-sex sexual relations are publicly stratified by differences in gender, the gender differences are highly correlated with differences in age.

There is also fascinating information here about what—as a sociolinguist raised on the work of Dell Hymes—I would call speech events and homosexual males' ways of communicating that are mostly nonverbal (chapter 8), as well as scrutiny of how *hombres* communicate desires they cannot (as proper men) speak (chapter 7). And—ironically for something written by someone so avowedly post-structuralist as Manuel Fernández-Alemany—there is a bravura structuralist analysis of kinds of male sexual human being in chapter 5.

The warring Enlightenment and Romantic strands within me make me ambivalent both to the AIDS-prevention missionaries pressing (or assuming) "modern gay" conceptions of homosexual oppression around the world and to the criticism of them in chapter 9, though I am unambivalently troubled by the homophobia carried by other kinds of zealot missionaries to Latin America.

I am interested in systematic observations of (homo)sexual cultures and acutely aware of the very limited data available about (homo)sexual subjectivities (having had to rely primarily on the literature of hostile alien observations in the travel and ethnography literatures that is the basis for my 2000 book *Homosexualities*), and was in contact with Manuel through most of his research and writing about the San Pedro Sula *ambiente*. encouraging him to try to make sense of the lifeways and worldviews of both "the homosexuals" and of their male sexual partners. But how did I become the coauthor of a book based on a dissertation that I did not even supervise? The tale is as complex as that of my non-visit to Honduras. The condensed answer is that moving on to intensive and long-term fieldwork in a remote lamasery in the Himalayas, Manuel told me that there was only going to be a book if I undertook transforming his dissertation into one. He insisted that I be bylined, not listed as the book's editor. I insisted that the body of the book remain in the first-person singular. The males he interviewed spoke to him, not to us, the observations and accounts of encountered are his, not ours. It would be both clumsy and dishonest to substitute "we" for "I." So how a book with two authors is written in the first-person singular is not as mysterious as it might seem.

There are sentences (beyond this preface) I have written, and I have rearranged his materials, but the data are entirely those gathered by Manuel Fernández-Alemany. So are the overwhelming majority of citations to published literature, including those to works written by me. There are certainly questions I would have liked to ask to those he interviewed (just as there are questions I wish I'd asked when I read transcripts of interviews I have conducted myself). Had I done the research, there would be more numbers and a focus on physical space, but I have learned to accept that, regrettably, other scholars never do exactly what I would like them to have done in their research, or what I imagine I would have done if I had been there. (This is a lesson that many social science book reviewers have failed to learn!) I hope that through our (serial) efforts, readers will learn something of the ongoing reproduction of traditional Latin American gendered asymmetric male-

male relations, whether this organization of embodied social differences persists or whether such accounts become historical artifacts.

—**Stephen O. Murray**
San Francisco, California
4 May 2002

PRELUDE

In August 1994 I went to Discotheque Terrazas, a cruisey place for people in the San Pedro Sula, the second-largest city in Honduras. Soon after I arrived there, an attractive young man approached me. He invited me to go upstairs, to the *terraza* or balcony, where we could have a soda and some fresh air and get away from the noisy and suffocating atmosphere of the disco's dancing area.

The encounter was flirtatious. I had the feeling that a sexual advance was inevitable after we both decided to go to the darker, more intimate *terraza* area. I was quite surprised, however, when he asked me, without previous introduction, explanation or apology: "How much are you going to pay me?"

"Pay you for what?"—I replied.

"Well," he said, "you are 'a homosexual' and I am not, so you must pay if you want to have sex with me." This was my first encounter with a Honduran *hombre* who has penetrative sex with homosexually identified males. Later I learned that this type of transaction was very common in *hombre*/homosexual relationships.

In a the second poorest country in Latin America (after Nicaragua), with a Gross Domestic Product (GDP) of US$650 per capita in 1992, the commodification of sex is prescriptive: *hombres* "must" get paid by homosexuals (especially effeminate *locas)* for access to their phalluses, although the *hombres* do not consider themselves to be engaging in prostitution, nor does it stigmatize them in the view of others as "homosexual."

A number of *hombres* who are underpaid, underemployed, or jobless, sustain themselves at least part of their living at the expense of *locas*. This is particularly true for younger *hombres*, like the ones I observed in Discotheque Terrazas, who frequent places that they know

1

they can find homosexuals willing to trade money for access to their erectile potency. This does not happen only in places like Discotheque Terrazas, known for being cruisey. It happens in lower-class neighborhood cantinas where *locas* buy *hombres* drinks by before going to bed with them.

1

INTRODUCTION

Masculine men in Latin America often publicly relate to effeminate, openly homosexual men in antagonistic ways, even
though, in private spaces, some of them lead intense emotional/sexual
relationships with a particular "homosexual." The field research
reported herein focuses on a heterogender type of sexual/romantic relationship that I observed among men of lower socioeconomic status in
San Pedro Sula, Honduras between 1994 and 1998. In these relationships, one of the men identifies as homosexual, while the other is simply an "*hombre*" (literally, a man) in his own self-image, self-
presentation, and general public perception.

Such relationships between phallic *hombres* and phallus-seeking, sex-
ually-receptive homosexuals seem to reproduce the power inequalities
attributed to patriarchal heterosexual relationships, although these
starkly asymmetrical relationships are idealized and actively pursued by
the "homosexuals" who willingly relinquish much male privilege.
Rather than label such relationships masculinist "oppression" and
"domination" or trot out the highly problematic contrast of "honor"
and "shame," an understanding is needed of the embodied social relationships and internalized culturally prescribed obligations and expectations for male-male sex in lower-class Latin American cities. What
French sociologist Pierre Bourdieu (2001:34) calls the "objectivity of
the subjective experience of relations of domination" and the rather
different conceptions *hombres* and homosexuals have of male-male sexual relationships in Honduras are the twin foci of this book.

3

Beginning with Simone de Beauvoir's pioneering, *The Second Sex* (1978[1949]), second-wave-feminists problematized the conflation of social gender and biological sex, often not considering sexuality at all (see the shifting critiques by Rubin 1975, 1984; and Butler 1990, 1993). In the pre-globalized sexual cultures of Latin America, a distinction between biological sex (having a penis) and gendered sexuality (using the penis to penetrate or being penetrated by men) is made, but biological sex is unimportant. The gender conflated with the sexuality is what is important. For lower-class males (not just in Honduras), gender and sexuality are so tightly interlinked that no distinction between them is routinely made. Heterosexual identity in men who (in etic perspective) regularly engage in homosexual intercourse follows a Latino cultural logic of gendered sexuality. It is not the effect of fragmented identities. The *hombre*/homosexual relationship is part of a gender/sexuality paradigm in which sexuality and gender are assumed to be, for all practical purposes, perfectly correlated. For Honduran males who have sex with males, *hombre* and *homosexual* are embodied statuses that shape conduct, not abstract intellectual conceptualizations.

Sexually penetrating another person is masculine/heterosexual, regardless of the biological (genital, chromosomal) sex of the person who is penetrated. Homosexual behavior does not imply homosexual identity in the case of the behaviorally bisexual male or *hombre*, because he is culturally marked as masculine. This gender/sexuality system has traditionally been maintained by taboos that prevent speaking publicly about sexuality in any serious manner. It also underlies pervasive hierarchies of gender/sexuality that mandate compulsory sexual passivity to effeminate homosexuals (who sometimes call themselves *locas*—"crazy girls") as well as to biological females, even though, as will be shown below, the categorization of males as *hombres* and homosexuals is somewhat variable as it is understood and enacted by different individuals and somewhat fluid over an individual's "sexual career." Moreover, there are some significant differences in the conception (and reported enactment) of the complementary roles as reported by *hombres* and by self-identified *locas*.

In their daily interaction, *hombres* and effeminate homosexuals have to cope with sometimes contradicting imperatives of cultural prescriptions and personal desires. This produces the commodification of desire, *hombre* feigning lack of interest and demanding "toll" charge," recurrent violence, territoriality; a complex inter-relation of teasing, contempt, and desire; as well as the need of *locas* to attract *hombre* attention by creating a scandal and by advertising sexual availability in other ways. Increasingly, as the last chapter will discuss, globalization processes and neoliberal economies have promoted and prescribed the appropriation of imagined (utopian) "modern" (North American) gay identities and complicated more traditional conceptions of gender nonconformity and homosexuality.

Roughly, from the 1990s on, however, with the increase in visibility of gay movements in Latin America, it has gradually become more evident that the politics of gender and the politics of sexuality have incompatible agendas. Homosexual groups that initially harbored gays, lesbians and transvestites now are dividing because of insurmountable tensions between these different sectors of the Latin American homosexual population. Lesbians do not feel that their issues as women are being properly addressed; gays do not like to be identified as transgendered by their association with transvestites; transvestites do not feel accepted as such, as they feel alienated from the masculinist appearance upheld as the "American" gay model (Murray 1996, 2000).

With the emergence of middle-class, assimilationist gay urban networks and gay activism, the first supported by an emerging neoliberal market, the latter supported by AIDS funding, it has become increasingly evident that lesbians, transvestites, and gays belong to different subcultures and fight for different rights. This has greatly affected the sexual politics of Latin America and the struggle against the AIDS epidemic (Klein 1998). AIDS money has been particularly aimed at men's issues and the decisions about the type of men to whom AIDS money should reach have been conservative, to say the least. New "gay" business has catered to masculine gay men, because these are the ones who can afford the commodities offered. Women and transgendered people have felt completely underrepresented in today's market of sexuality where AIDS-Inc. and neoliberalism play a prominent role. Class cannot be ignored. In Latin America most full-time transvestites are commercial sex workers who belong to the lower SES (Prieur 1998:150). Those identifying as "gays" tend to belong to middle and upper-middle socioeconomic statuses, hold more conservative jobs and be "closeted" (151; Murray 1995:145-49, 2000:408-12).

Fieldwork in San Pedro Sula

In 1993, while doing post-graduate study in anthropology at the University of Southern California, I was also volunteering at an AIDS agency in Hollywood. There I met a few Hondurans who told me about their country. I reviewed the literature on homosexuality in Latin America and I found that nothing had been published on homosexuality in Honduras. There were a few publications about Guatemala, Nicaragua, Costa Rica, and other countries, but nothing about Honduras. In the summer of 1994 I was able to travel to Honduras and spent about a month there. In San Pedro Sula, a city close to the Atlantic coast of Honduras, I met several people who were part of a homosexual local culture.

I was told that violence against homosexual people was all too frequent. Even coming from Los Angeles, I felt an extraordinarily palpable degree of violence in the environment, not only against homosexuals but in general. This feeling was reinforced by what the people I met recounted.

Miguel Ángel Lemus, the first homosexually identified person in Honduras whom I met, I found through the Damron international gay tourist guide, in which he was listed as a contact person.[1] Miguel was

---

1.   Unfortunately, Miguel died due to complications related to AIDS in 1997.

very well known in town because he was the owner of the popular bar El Corcel Negro, and openly homosexual. Miguel was extremely helpful in showing me the homosexual "scene" in San Pedro Sula, which at that time seemed to be centered on El Corcel Negro. Indeed, Miguel's bar was the only locale in town that was identified by many as a quasi-gay place—"quasi-" because the clientele was mixed.

El Corcel was located in Medina, a lower-middle socioeconomic status neighborhood in San Pedro "below the line." Traditionally (and symbolically), San Pedro has been divided into two halves marked by the railroad line: below the line, where the poor live and above the line, where the rich live. Most of my fieldwork was done "below the line." Because of an increase in gang activity, most Sanpedrans considered the area "below the line" dangerous. Miguel lived just one block away from El Corcel and I spent the last two weeks of my trip staying in Miguel's home and working as a bartender at El Corcel.

Miguel introduced me to several of his lovers, who were young men, usually in their teens, who also lived in the same neighborhood. Miguel gave them free drinks, treated them well, and usually ended up having sex with them the same night. These men did not think of themselves as homosexuals but simply as men (*hombres*). That they were having sex with Miguel did not lead them to question their masculinity/heterosexuality. They were "masculine" by Honduran standards and played the insertor's role during anal intercourse. It is important to note that these *hombres* were very young, still unmarried. In Honduran (and other Latin American) society, unmarried men have greater sexual freedom than do married men, and much more than married or unmarried women do. For a man to penetrate a homosexual is seen as a peccadillo, probably worse than getting drunk, but about as bad as getting high on marijuana. As with other peccadilloes, young men may indulge in them as long as they are sufficiently discreet about it, so as not to offend public decency (see Prieur 1998:196).

Miguel, on the other hand, was openly a *loca*, which meant that he was penetrated by men and not fully a man (*un hombre*) himself in the cultural view of masculinity in which having a penis is irrelevant. As a *loca*, Miguel could have been criticized by some people as immoral or lewd, but in general he was much liked by his neighbors. More than his sexuality, what seemed to matter to Miguel's neighbors was Miguel's friendliness, generosity, and willingness to help people. Sometimes this friendliness with Miguel, especially coming from male neighbors, seemed to mingle with sexual desire, as I remember seeing mature, married men smiling at Miguel from their homes as they grabbed their crotches in a suggestive and inviting manner. (These men and Miguel had lived in the neighborhood for decades, and many of these men had had sexual intercourse with Miguel in the past.)

Through Miguel, I met other homosexually identified men, and formally interviewed several of them, including Miguel.

The more I became involved with the homosexual subculture in San Pedro Sula, the more people around me felt compelled to classify me as either an *hombre* or a *loca*.[2] I had to be assigned to a side. When I met him, I told Miguel Lemus that I was "gay." However, gay in its more "modern" conception, didn't exist or was almost nonexistent during my first trip to Honduras. The word *gay* was very rarely used, and, when it was used, it was another label for being a *loca*—without any new or different meaning. For Miguel, *gay* was a synonym of *loca*, so he didn't conceive that I might not like to be treated as a woman-like creature by *hombres*. This was clear in the dance-floor of his bar (El Corcel Negro), where the dances were only between *hombres* and *locas*, or between *hombres* and loose women (usually prostitutes). Dancing involved both bodies being attached to each other in a tight embrace in which one could either take the man's or the woman's role. I felt that the *hombres* forced me to take the woman's role. I tried to take the man role, (which implied leading the steps and also holding the other's hand rather than letting the other holding one's), but it became a ludi-

---

2.   *Loca* is the feminine form of "crazy person." It connotes a cultural view that it is crazy to give up the rewards of manhood for the dubious pleasures of being sexually penetrated.

crous struggle, and I was always eventually overpowered and put in place: the subordinate homosexual place. During slow, romantic ballads, the *hombres* would hold me around the waist and push my arms up to their shoulders. By trying to define myself as a homosexual who likes a other homosexuals ("gay"), *locas* considered me as a *traca*, but *traca* ultimately is a kind of *loca* and not an *hombre* in the primary dichotomization of male human beings. Trying to be "gay" in the modern/international sense or a *traca* in the local elaboration of roles (discussed in chapter 5), I was seen as being a kind of *loca*—even if a more restrained and "ladylike" one than many of the *loca* friends I made who gleefully emulated "loose women" in "sluttishly" provocative dress and demeanor.

Being cast as a *loca,* made me uncomfortable dealing with *hombres,* but also let me quickly into the homosexual subculture (*ambiente*) as a quasi-insider.[3] Regarded as being a *loca,* dealing with these *hombres* in my work as a bartender and in other social settings (such as going out to Discotheque Terrazas, for example) made me feel subordinate to swaggering phallus-wielders. These penetrating (phallic) men were irreverent, rude at times, even ruthless. They treated *locas* as sexual objects. To them, *locas* were just below or at the same level of the categories of "easy" woman and female prostitute.

Throughout my research I was frequently asked, "Why Honduras?" Most of the time I have felt compelled to answer, "Why **not** Honduras?" Honduras has remained largely unstudied by anthropologists interested in doing contemporary urban ethnography. Perhaps the fact that Honduras does not have a tradition of social movements of resistance to Euroamerican neocolonialist capitalism to the degree of Guatemala, Nicaragua or El Salvador, has made Honduras less interesting to many who study social change. Moreover, the fact that Honduras has to a great extent been the backyard of the United States, where not

---

3.   On the advantages and disadvantages of insider perspectives see Merton 1972.

only bananas, but also Cold War counterinsurgency bases have grown, has made of Honduras a place not very appealing for many.

My interest in the lower-class Honduran homosexual *ambiente* went from serendipity and initial curiosity to a growing fascination for a local tradition of gender-stratified sexuality that brought issues of gender/sexual identity to extremes I have never seen before anywhere else in an urban Latin American setting. Moreover, the high levels of male violence and male power display that I observed in Honduras made me interested in exploring how "the power of the phallus" was related to the particularities of this sexual culture.

After extraordinarily charged experiences during my first visit to Honduras, I returned to Los Angeles to begin my Ph.D. studies at the University of Southern California. I was still not sure about my dissertation topic, but after writing a paper I presented at a gay and lesbian studies conference held at USC in the spring of 1995, I was positive that I wanted to do my dissertation on the sexual culture I had begun to observe in Honduras. I romantically entitled the paper "*Las locas*: Third-gender oppression and resistance in Honduras." My initial research question centered on the issue of violence and heterosexual male supremacy. I used the Marxist/Gramscian paradigm of societal structures of oppression and resistance in which heterosexual men oppressed *locas* and women as a group. I was committed to finding ways to defuse violence from the standpoint of a gay Latin American scholar using an applied, advocacy/action anthropological approach (as in Sears and Williams 1997).

I went to Honduras again in 1996. This time I especially focused on violence against homosexual people, especially in the forms of murder and physical assault, that was perpetrated against the transgendered sector of the homosexual population, and especially against transgendered sexual workers. Most of the cases of murder against homosexuals reported in Honduras were cases of transgendered prostitutes killed on the streets, late at night. Honduran authorities' homophobia was obvious in their indifference and lack of follow-up in these cases.

In 1996 the first report on the violation of human rights of sexual minorities and people living with HIV/AIDS in Honduras was published (Elliott 1996a). Building on this, I realized that if I wanted to deal with the topic of violence, I should either focus on street transgendered prostitutes or I should approach violence in a broader way. I also realized that I needed to problematize the concept of "violence."

During my 1997 fieldwork, I decided that although I was still going to investigate violence, it was not going to be the central theme of my research. By then I was increasingly interested in studying the sexual culture as a whole and wanted to avoid a reductionist violence approach. I have tried to credit *locas'* and *hombres'* agency. My thesis is that **both** partners are actively affected by and affect these relationships, which at the same time are shaped by and maintain (reproduce) local sexual cultures. Only later, after my 1998 fieldwork, did I fully realize that the *hombre/loca* relationship is only possible within a culture in which gender and sexuality are indivisible in practice.

I was also influenced by poststructuralist perspectives that challenge the adequacy of models of vertical power through which the relationship oppressor/oppressed is established. This perspective sees power as immanent and in constant reproduction due to the individual and collective agency and embodied practices of the people exercising it, not just imposed from above (see Foucault 1978; Bourdieu 1980; Wolf 1999).

Some authors have argued that heterosexual men oppress women and homosexual men as a group. Poststructuralism problematizes this thesis by thinking of power in forms that are fluidly interactive rather than rigid and vertical. Thus, it is necessary to question a current paradigm in the study of masculinities based on structural ideas of oppression: "hegemonic" masculinities vs. "subordinate" masculinities (see Donaldson 1993). Within the structuralist paradigm, the contrast between circum-Mediterranean and Protestant ethics has brought important issues of discourse and public disclosure of information about sexual behavior (and ontology) into consideration. David Gilmore (1990:30-55) provides the best introduction to a circum-Mediterranean model of masculinity and gender in cultures. Stephen Murray—in his works on homosexuality in Latin America (1987, 1995) and in Muslim cultures (1997)—embraces to a point this Weberian distinction. Whitam and Mathy (1986) do as well, though they underestimate the extent to which a Iberian colonialism that lasted longer in the Philippines than in Latin America makes the former as well as the latter an area away from the Mediterranean with a substantial Mediterranean—and specifically Roman Catholic—cultural heritage.

It has been claimed that in a Protestant society people's lives should be virtuous and transparent and there should be no contradiction between the inside and the outside (Weber 1958[1904-5]). People's virtue requires that even their more intimate acts should follow similar rules to their public behavior, because "you are what you do." In a Mediterranean(culture-influenced) society, on the other hand, a marked distinction between the more public and the more private should be the norm. People are allowed to do many things in private that they should not mention, still less publicize. Sexuality is one of these things. Making public one's sexuality shows that one has extremely poor manners, at best, or is an antisocial, at worst. Public decency becomes an imperative feature of civility. People's "sins" are condoned as long as the perpetrators do not talk about them. To make things easier, people will simulate not having perceived improper acts and they will not ask or press for revelations (unseemly public confessions).

The deployment of rigid categorization established by imaginary borders, however, risks reifying structures and overlooking the complex historical interconnectedness that made it possible for these differences to develop in the first place (cf. Parker 1999). In addition, Latin and Anglophone American cultural roots are very diverse and cannot be delimited to and neatly classified as circum-Mediterranean and Protestant ethic paradigms. Cultural influences in Latin and Anglophone America have often formed a mosaic of cultural features. Catholicism is not unimportant in Canada and the United States, and Protestant evangelism is increasingly influential in Central America. Moreover, recent changes in Latin American societies due to the globalization of the economy and culture as part of neoliberalist trends and telecommunications have accelerated cultural change in Latin America and transformed and hybridized identities.[4] As Gutmann (1996:14) cautioned, "There is not a Mexican or Latin or Spanish-speaking cultural system of generally agreed-upon gender meanings and experience.... Gender identities...are products and manifestations of cultures in motion; they do not emanate from some primordial essence whose resilience bears testament to perpetual forms of inequality."

Nevertheless, there is at least one difference that seems very important to me: the emphasis and insistence of Anglophone academia in verbalizing private acts, which resembles Protestant testimonials about lives of sin and subsequent salvation. This emphasis has created much tension in studies of sexuality in Catholic Latin America, where confession (and sexuality) have traditionally belonged to more private spheres. Although confession is more Catholic than Protestant, Catholic confessions occur in dyadic interactions for which there is a seal of secrecy. The boundary between a dyadic relationship in which forbidden knowledge is known-about and public reticence about acknowledging "private" behavior is less permeable in San Pedro than in Anglo circles in the United States.

---

4. See Fernández-Alemany 1999, Fernández-Alemany and Sciolla 1999; Carrillo 1999, 2002.

Methods

My fieldwork involved a total of nine months unevenly distributed into four visits to Honduras: three weeks in 1994, one week in 1996, four months in 1997, and four months in 1998.

The study was based on interviews and participant observation, triangulating self-reports with what I observed and personally experienced.[5] My participant observation during social interactions, such as parties and social meetings depended upon my access through personal relationships and through the NGO "Comunidad Gay Sampedrana." Some interviews were formal and semi-structured, others informal and non-structured. The formal or semi-structured interviews lasted between one and two hours each and were recorded. I was especially interested in how stories about relationships differ between *hombres* and *locas* and strove to find connections between *hombres'* and *locas'* perceptions of sexuality and gender and how these affected and were affected the way they lived. Questions were generally open-ended, although I followed some standard techniques of in-depth interviewing (Eyre 1997). I took photographs of the interviewees and of people in social settings as well.

I interviewed 34 men who have sex with men. Informally I interviewed 20 (8 homosexually identified and 12 heterosexually identified). Formally I interviewed 14 men (7 homosexually identified and 7 heterosexually identified), one person, Osvaldo, twice. In total I inter-

---

5.   Some have called this "the Bolton method" after the frank advocacy of Bolton (1992). Participant observation in sex causes consternation among many anthropologists who show no similar concern about anthropologists eating food that badly nourished research subjects share with them. As of spring 2002, the American Anthropology Association's ethics committee—a group that signally fails to address ethical problems in what it directly controls (its professional journals)—is attempting to legislate sexual conduct "in the field" (any society). See the sensible discussion of having sex with those whose sexual culture is being studied in Murray 1996b and Carrier 1999, and the more general reflection of Wax 1980.

viewed 19 heterosexually identified and 15 homosexually identified men who have sex with men.[6]

The age range for the 19 interviewees of heterosexual identity was between 15 and 26, with a median age of 21. They were (pseudonyms, ordered by age), José Pantín, 15-16; Alexander David, 17; Jaime, 18; Gerson Donali, 19; Freddie, 19; Enrique, 21; and Allan Geovanny, 22 (formal interviews); and Dimitri, 15; Marlon, ca.18; Rivereño, 20; Julio, 21; El Turco, 22; Rigo, 22; Eduardo, 23; Joel A., 23; Héctor C., ca. 24; Alfredo J., ca. 24; Marvin, 25; and Héctor M., 26 (informal interviews).

The age range for the 15 interviewees of homosexual identity was between 18 and 72, with a median age of 29. They were (pseudonyms, ordered by age), Saskia, 24; Osvaldo, 30; Fausto, 33; Horacio, 38; Miguel, 44; Mango, 55; and Don Pedro, 72 (formal interviews); and Wilson, 18; Antonio, ca. 22; Charlie, ca. 22; Luigi, ca. 25, Elmer, 29; Carioca, 30; Cindy, ca. 35; and Helvecio, ca. 50 (informal interviews).

The age differences between the two categories is consistent with the cultural belief, my personal observation, and other social scientists' findings that the young bisexual partners with heterosexual identities abandons homosexual behavior when he is about 25, while the man of homosexual identity maintains his identity, behavior and desire

---

6.   Besides the 34 men who have sex with men interviewed, I interviewed six gay-identified representatives of four different gay organizations in Honduras, one of whom was a lesbian-identified woman (Nina Cobos). These interviews did not deal with "personal" issues, like the other interviews did, but focused on general themes related to sexuality, gender and gay human rights in Honduras. In addition, due to class, residence or gender status, some of the people interviewed here did not participate of the fieldwork setting in which my research took place. The interviews of the openly gay activists were published (Fernández-Alemany and Larson 1996) and I use the interviewees' real names, The six interviewees were: Jesús Guillén, from the Asociación Hondureña de Homosexuales y Lesbianas Contra el Sida, in San Pedro Sula; Alfredo Idiáquez and Juan José Zambrano, from Colectivo Violeta, in Tegucigalpa; Nina Cobos, from Prisma, in Tegucigalpa; and Evelio Pineda and Dereck Raickov, from Comunidad Gay Sampedrana, in San Pedro Sula.

throughout his life (e.g., Whitam 1992; Carrier 1995; Murray 1995:50-54; Prieur 1998:214, 234; Fernández-Alemany and Sciolla 1999). What sociologists (e.g., Turner 1978) call "role-self merger" is into a homosexual self for the penetrated male, into a masculine self (not implicated in homosexuality) for the penetrators.

Persuading heterosexually identified *hombres* to speak about their homosexual behavior is not an easy task.[7] Their use of males as sexual "outlets" (to borrow Kinsey's term) belongs to the realm of the private, of things that may be done but should not spoken about ("Todos hecho, nada dicho").

Some, such as Paul Kutsche (1995) believe "sexual anarchy" or a "happy limbo of a non-identity" (Butler 1990: 100) occur in Latin America when males engage in homosexual behavior (both receptive and insertive) while resisting any kind of homosexually related identity at all.[8] In this cultural context, struggling to make *hombres* "confess" their homosexual acts in an interview is not only an imperialist and alien imposition on them, but also a cultural oxymoron, since if they cannot speak about something, then, at least publicly, it does not exist. As Murray (2000:271) put it: "There are elaborate collusions to avoid questioning in public appearances, even those that could easily be challenged, and to preclude noticing deviance—in gender, sexual behavior, or other kinds." This is the first great methodological obstacle one is

---

7.   Researchers such as Carrier (1995:198, 205) and Kulick (1996:n5) met great obstacles trying to interview these men and to get them to tell even a fraction of their homosexual experiences. Prieur (1998) was able to interview some bisexuals (behaviorally bisexual, not bisexual-identifying). Most of them, however, denied having had homosexual experiences, although Prieur knew they were not being accurate (190-92, 199). Likewise, Gutmann (1996) was only able to gather extremely limited data on the homosexual experiences of the men he interviewed in Mexico City (only one admitted to any).

8.   Gay scholars native to Latin America such as Luiz Mott (1995 and in multiple publications in Portuguese) and Jacobo Schifter (1989 et seq.) have challenged the exoticizing picture of polymorphous perversity without labels or violence against "perverts" such as Kutsche's "sexual anarchy" and Parker's "no sin south of the equator" effusions.

faced with in this type of interview, especially with *hombres. Locas*, on the other hand, sometimes are more than willing to speak about their homosexual behavior and that of others—if questions are asked in the proper context.[9]

Prieur (1998) and Kulick and Willson (1995) pose an interesting question: what can the researcher learn from what is *not* said? Erasures in representation may provide valuable information about the sexual culture studied, although this requires reading between lines. I tried to follow Annick Prieur's example. When her interviewees did not want to cooperate or were contradictory in what they were saying, rather than trying to press them to disclose accurate information, she focused on these limits and contradictions in themselves: "I made these limits my object of research: they are far more interesting than what I possibly could have made my subjects admit by pressuring. The discrepancies between what I saw and what I heard are very indicative, and have helped me to understand the sensitive nature of several topics.... They may have many reasons for not telling, maybe for not even admitting to themselves" (1998:23).

Fortunately, and to my surprise, I found that most of the (behaviorally) bisexual men I interviewed were willing to tell me about their homosexual experiences and what they felt during them. During my fieldwork I learned that the best way to interview people resistant to being interviewed and speak with them about what is difficult to speak about was by contacting them through the social networks in which

---

9.   A similar pattern was described in pre-gay-liberation homosexual life in North America by Leznoff 1956, Burdick and Yvette. 1974, Warren 1977. In a note (33) limiting to public space the statement I quoted from Murray (2000:271), he clarified, "Gossip among *pasivos* is incessant (and *pasivos* hang out together when they are not snaring and bedding the *activos* who travel solo and do not hang out with each other). Aspersions of how masculine and impenetrable another *pasivo*'s partner really is are especially common, though some are surely based entirely on spite rather than actual experience with the particular male whose masculine credentials are challenged (in his absence)." This phenomenon is discussed in chapter 8 below as "drama" in the Honduran *loca* context.

they were involved with people of alternative masculinities. Therefore my access to the private world of the bisexual male was through the one who best knows what the bisexual male does with a male in private: his homosexual partner. In addition, besides being a native Spanish speaker, I had multiple insider status as a male, as a Latin American native speaker of Spanish, and as a participant observer who lived among voluble *locas* with wide experience of navigating sexual relationships with masculine-identified *hombres*.[10]

Plan of the book

Chapter 2 offers a sociohistorical introduction to the city of San Pedro Sula. I show how the feelings of danger and violence in which gender and sexual relations are embedded in San Pedro are deeply rooted in the cultural and geographical memory of the region in which disease, natural disasters, and violence have been endemic for centuries.

Chapter 3 discusses how sexuality has been traditionally kept out of most public discourses in Latin America, finding its way to public forms only through joking and double-entendre-making. This chapter shows how the venerable taboo against talking seriously about sex has hindered the development of a homosexual identity among subjects of a masculine gender identification.

---

10. However, I had no experience of such traditional rigid gender dichotomization as I encountered in Honduras. In Chile I felt I was an outsider, because I didn't fit in mainstream young guys' interests, like sports and dating women, but I didn't have a gay identity, and I didn't have sex with males or participate in the local gay subculture. In my native city of Santiago, Chile the macho/homosexual relationship is inconspicuous. It is regarded as old-fashioned and rural . After I had come out in Los Angeles, I interviewed two pairs of Chileans who were in that type of relationship. I was referred to them by some friends of mine as something special, the kind of vanishing phenomenon with which anthropologists are supposed to be interested. Since both of the macho partners of the gays I interviewed were rural men, so it reinforced my perception of rural, backward, obsolete gender dichotomization.

The following three chapters lay out the ideologies of man-male penetration in Honduras (and other lower-class "traditional" Latin American settings), beginning with discussion of the norms (regarded as pregiven by nature) that men cannot be penetrated and homosexuals cannot penetrate.

Native categorization of sexual roles and characters in the homosexual *ambiente* are an important part of this sexual culture and important for orienting attempts to connect with others (particular species of sexual beings) in ways not leading to shocked and violent reactions. "Categories" are not only intellectual abstractions but organize sociosexual practices. Chapters 5 and 6 show that these categorizations are more fluid than the simplistic ideological dichotomies. Through time, and depending on differing viewpoints, the same person may move back and forth between and through two or more of these categories.

Chapter 5 lays out the typology of kinds of males who have sex with males that the effeminate homosexuals believe in and act upon. Chapter 6 investigates the views of their sexuality held by the young men who penetrate homosexuals (the *hombres*). Although the fundamental penetrator/penetratee model is shared by both the "homosexuals" and their "heterosexual" male partners, there are substantial differences between the two about what men desire about the bodies and in the public appearances of the homosexual partners. Chapter 6 also challenges the flimsily based claims that penetrating a male increases the penetrator's standing as a hypermasculine embodiment of male honor.

The following two chapters describe some of the ways in which *hombres* and *locas* signal their interest, feign disinterest, keep their affairs invisible to those not in-the-know (*los entendidos*), and sometimes throw caution and discretion to the winds.

Chapter 7 analyzes the relationship between the *hombre* and the *loca* from multiple angles: the commodification of desire and the games of not showing interest played by the *hombre*; tolls charged *locas* for being in public (i.e., *hombre*) space, the complex equation of teasing, contempt, and desire. Payments to the *hombre* not only disguise *hombre* desire for sex with a male, it is also part of a system of gender inequality that benefits the *hombre* in many other respects. The public representation of *locas* as exclusively passive is related to hierarchies of power and gender inequality which construct sexual passivity in *locas* (and heterosexual passivity in women) as the only natural options, making *locas* and women sexually available for *hombres*, the penetrators. Despite the seemingly obvious power implications of compulsory passivity in feminine men, many *locas* seem very much to desire to be penetrated and to be willing to mark themselves as feminine in order to attract penetrators.

Chapter 8 presents (1) *picardía*—ways of speaking in public about homosexual interests in ways that those not familiar with the homosexual *ambiente* do not understand, (2) the dramatic exaggeration that is appreciated inside the homosexual *ambiente*, and (3) the occasional explosion of flaunting sexual availability (the last the obverse of the discretion of *picardía*). While *locas* sometimes actively pursue creating a scandal to be acknowledged, and desired and many times choose to mark themselves as feminine to attract *hombres* who may want to sexually penetrate them, the *loca* often must play by the rules of the *hombre* regarding territory and must tolerate being teased and shaken-down if he does not want to be physically attacked by the *hombres*.

In Chapter 9, I argue that sexuality in Honduras (as elsewhere in Latin America) has been commodified as part of neoliberalist globalization as well as in the spread of fundamentalist Protestant churches. This has facilitated the development of a new gay identity based on a marketed model of individualist, consumerist, and masculinist "American" gay man. Although the appearance of AIDS exacerbated homophobia, because people blamed homosexuals for the epidemic, AIDS eventually became a key factor in the emergence of the gay social movement in Honduras by bringing funding to newly formed gay AIDS organizations. Encouraged, in part, by international funding guidelines, these groups embraced stereotypical "American" models. The commercialization and appropriation of these imagined American gay models has alienated women and transgendered people from gay and lesbian activism while it has empowered a sector that benefits from the marketing of AIDS and the "American" gay lifestyle. The "American" gay model has empowered those who have sought to liberate themselves from more traditional gender/sexuality strictures, yet also simultaneously provoking a reactive homophobia, as the "American"-mirroring, gender conforming, and outspoken gay or lesbian has threatened traditional gender conceptions and violated previously established norms of proper behavior in public spheres. These new gay identities and meanings of "gay" have conflicted and continue to compete, hybridize, and relexify with more traditional conceptions of gender nonconformity and homosexuality, creating meanings which are multiple, contradictory, and in constant negotiation in this era of neoliberalism, globalization, and imagined "American ways." Chapter 9 also considers a tension between paternalism and liberalism, which is present throughout the book.

2

THE LAND OF PESTILENCE

This chapter voices a feeling shared by many Sanpedrans that their city has been built on tough lands where natural disasters, disease, and violence have made life difficult for its inhabitants. My own experience during my fieldwork of "the land of pestilence" included losing to AIDS deaths two important participants of my research, being attacked twice by robbers (and suffering many other failed attempts), becoming sick with an unknown tropical disease, and survived the especially devastating hurricane named Mitch.

San Pedro's population almost disappeared several times across Honduran history and the city has had to be rebuilt on repeated occasions after natural disasters. Malaria and other tropical diseases have been endemic to San Pedro for centuries. To make things worse, today San Pedro Sula is the heart of the AIDS epidemic in Central America with a pattern similar to the one found in Central Africa. Torture and other violations of human rights by the military were commonplace during the 1980s. Street violence, urban youth gangs, and the use of guns by civilians as self-defense have been out of control since the early 1990s. The violence in San Pedro and Tegucigalpa, the capital city, was becoming so bad that in November of 1998 the Honduran government imposed a national curfew and sent the army into the streets. There are numerous precedents of disaster in San Pedro.

Spaniards first arrived to the Sula Valley, near the northern coast of what today is Honduras, in 1523. The Spanish Conquistador Pedro de

Alvarado founded San Pedro de Sula either in April (Stone 1954:113) or on June 27 (UIES 1993:13; Pastor Fasquelle 1990:73) of 1536. He founded the city in the beautiful and green Sula Valley close to two major rivers, the Chamelecón and the Ulúa, in the foothills of the El Merendón mountain range, which, with its lush tropical rain forest, still provides a striking backdrop to the city.

The Spanish Crown declared San Pedro Sula the capital of the province of Honduras within the Kingdom of Guatemala. In 1573, however, governor don Diego de Herrera moved the capital to Comayagua without waiting for the Crown's consent, because he could not stand the humid heat of the Sula Valley (Stone 1954:139-40). Many of the inhabitants of San Pedro also left.

At the time of the conquest in 1523, the Sula Valley had about 50,000 (PastorFasquelle 1990). By 1575, San Pedro had only 50 Spaniards left and about 3,000 natives scattered through 30 hamlets around the city. In only 42 years the indigenous population had decreased in number 94 percent, primarily due to newly introduced diseases. A Spanish official who visited San Pedro in 1575 declared: "it's a very sick population...but the land is fertile, with much corn, cocoa, honey, beeswax, many cows and mares and the complete livestock from Spain" (López de Velasco [1971]: 301-306 in Pastor Fasquelle 1990:103).

Spaniards quickly learned that nothing could be built to last under the Sula Valley's copious rains and above it devastating floods: "everything built throughout a year would be destroyed in one single day of rain" (unknown chronicler, cited in Pastor Fasquelle 1990:104), as is vividly shown in Peter Weir's 1986 film of Paul Theroux's novel *Mosquito Coast* in which the family members manage to survive by climbing onto an improvised raft—a situation not much different from what many Hondurans experienced during hurricane Mitch in 1998.

In 1589-90 there were only 20 hamlets left and there were fewer than 500 people living in the area. By 1629 only ten people remained (Pastor Fasquelle 1990:103-04). In addition to the plagues and floods, there was devastation caused by pirate attacks. Almost no Spanish ship could escape the pirates in Honduran waters after 1634, so the Crown suspended trade along the Honduran northern coast and eventually throughout the entire Central American coast (112). British pirates ransacked San Pedro Sula, and in 1660 San Pedro was completely destroyed by the pirate François De Olonais (Stone 1954: 145).

San Pedro was refounded ca. 1682 in a different part of the Sula Valley. Later, after being destroyed by another flood, the city was established one the *loca*tion that is now the central business district of San Pedro. Because of San Pedro's more recent increase in size, however, the three main *loca*tions where San Pedro was founded are all encompassed by today's city (Pastor Fasquelle 1990: 119). However, for two hundred years the population grew very little. The area of the Sula Valley remained isolated and disease-ridden. San Pedro had become a tiny village of smugglers who hid from the law in the rain forest (UIES 1993: 18). Between 1872 and 1894 the city experienced major changes: increasing immigration and a railway connection to other parts of the country. By 1888, three centuries after its foundation, San Pedro had only 1,714 inhabitants (19). San Pedro's ethnic makeup was *mestizo* (mixed) with cultural and genetic backgrounds deriving from Africa, Europe, Meso-America and the Caribbean.

Between 1895 and 1919 banana plantations developed in Honduras. Integration into the world market accelerated urban growth. By 1900 the city had 5,000 inhabitants, and by 1920. more than 10,000 (UIES 1993:19).

Although a flourishing cash crop market, the banana business created a dependency between Honduras and major transnational US-based corporations, a dependency that was particularly clear during the Cold War years when the US established military bases in Honduras, like the Pomarola base in Comayagua, and trained people to fight the Sandinista in Nicaragua. The CIA was complicit with or directly sponsored many of the violations against human rights perpetrated in Honduras during the 1980s (Bowman 1999: 11).

Between 1914 and 1974 the Sula Valley and northern coast of Honduras was hit by four hurricanes, the last three of them coming exactly after a 20 year lapse (1914, 1934, 1954, and 1974). When hurricane Fifí hit the Honduran coast on September 14, 1974 nobody seemed prepared (Grupo Editorial 1989:127). The consequences were disastrous: about 20 villages completely disappeared, and 10,000 people died, many of them in Choloma, only a 20-minute drive from San Pedro Sula (125-26). When the still more devastating hurricane Mitch stalled over Honduras in 1998, hundreds of thousands were evacuated from the higher-risk areas, like Choloma, there were still close to 6,000 deaths. Had people not evacuated and prepared this time, the deaths might have surpassed the hundreds of thousands.

In 1985 the first case of AIDS was reported in the city, and the number of cases quickly multiplied. San Pedro became sadly known as "la capital del SIDA" (the capital city of AIDS). By March 1998, with only 17 percent of Central America's population, Honduras had 50 percent of the total of AIDS cases reported for Central America (García Trujillo, Paredes, and Sierra 1998:12). Most of these cases came from the Sula Valley region.

In the prostitution area of Suncery, sanitary authorities shut down "El Gay," the only gay bar in San Pedro, along with many brothels. After El Gay was shut, El Corcel Negro in Barrio Medina became the hangout for people who wanted to meet other people of alternative sexualities.

The reasons why San Pedro Sula became the capital of AIDS remain mysterious. Some think it must be the inevitable outcome for a cursed land, the land of pestilence. The most plausible hypothesis claims that AIDS spread so quickly in the Sula Valley because of the great numbers of foreign military and the prostitution that grew around their bases. The HIV virus then spread out to the rest of the population due to promiscuity, bisexuality, and unprotected sex practices common across the Sanpedran sexual landscape. As García Trujillo, Paredes, and Sierra wrote:

With the victory of Sandinism in Nicaragua, Central America, especially Honduras, became the core of the Cold War in the Americas. It has been claimed that the heavy presence of foreign troops in Honduras was associated with an increase in prostitution and STDs precisely in the towns where the military bases were located and in the leisure areas visited by the military. According to official reports, gonorrhea cases increased from 143 per 100,000 inhabitants in 1979 to 196 per 100,000 inhabitants in 1984. A similar increase was observed in syphilis: 69 cases per 100,000 inhabitants in 1979; 111 cases per 100,000 inhabitants in 1984. (1998:12)

Sexually transmitted diseases that create open ulcers in the genital area, like syphilis, make it easier for the HIV virus to enter the blood stream and infect the person.

Street violence has dramatically increased since the early 1990s. From about 1993 on, and especially after Proposition 187 was approved by California voters in 1994, the US government has been massively deporting Hondurans from cities like Los Angeles back to Honduras. Many of these deportees were young men and women, children of undocumented, underpaid workers. As their parents had to work double shifts to make ends meet and be able to save some money to send back to Honduras, these children grew up underattended and spent much of their time on the streets (Vigil and Yun 1996: 150-51, 155). Many of these children joined one of the two major Latino youth gangs in Los Angeles, rebelling against racial discrimination by Mexican-Americans (Ward, lecture of January 28, 1999 at USC): M.S., or "Mara Salvatrucha" (originally a Salvadoran-American gang) and "La 18," or "18th Street." With the involuntary arrival of many Los Angeles gang members, San Pedro rapidly became a gang-infested city. A new "disease" had been added to a long list of calamities, this time imported directly from the US. Other US-imported youth gangs made their appearance, too, like "Los Vatos Locos," and the *mara* or gang "Mao-Mao."[1]

San Pedro's most affected area was the southeast, also called area #4. Two important neighborhoods in this area of town are Barrio Medina and Barrio Cabañas, the two *barrios* where I conducted most of my fieldwork. Southeast San Pedro is also the area where AIDS hit with the most virulence, where the brothel sector of Suncery is *loca*ted, and where the *hombre/loca* relationship is most prevalent. Cabañas and Suncery are areas of lower socioeconomic status. Medina, a little bit higher up in the social "scale," is predominantly middle-low socioeconomic status. Medina is where most automobile mechanic shops are, where El Corcel Negro was located, and where I stayed in my visits of 1994 and 1996, before I moved to Barrio Cabañas. The main street market of San Pedro is also in Medina.

For eight months during 1997 and 1998 I lived in Barrio Cabañas. On the corner across from where I stayed is the "headquarters" of mara Mao-Mao, the dominant youth gang in Cabañas. Shooting could be heard almost every night. One night a stray bullet perforated the roof of our house and lodged in my host's hammock right after he stepped out of it to go to the bathroom.

Fear of street violence, robbery, and rape was becoming so prevalent among civilians that they began arming themselves. By the end of my fieldwork in 1998 it was a common sight to see men carrying guns, which were not concealed at all, but were displayed with bravado. Men usually stuck the pistol in the front of their pants, pointing towards their crotch. For example, my host's brother, newly arrived back in Honduras after years of working undocumented in Miami, "had" to carry a revolver above his crotch to protect his car from being stolen. (Nevertheless, the car was stolen anyway a few months later). I saw men who exchanged dollars for Lempiras (Honduras' currency) at San Pedro's International Airport while they were carelessly playing with their pistols in front of the tourists. I also saw my host's nephew of only

---

1.   Similar reports of an alarming increase in gang violence following the massive deportation of undocumented youth in Los Angeles and other US cities has also been reported for Honduras' neighbor, El Salvador (DeCesare 1998).

18 playing on the street with his uncle's gun. On several occasions I scolded one of the people who collaborated on the research project with me, because he would let his teenaged and emotionally immature lover play with his loaded gun in my presence. The tradition of men carrying—, however, is not new and men armed with machetes have long been commonplace in San Pedro.

Beginning in the 1990s San Pedro also experienced an economic boom as a consequence of the business of *maquiladoras*—commonly known as "*maquilas*"—, which are clothing assembling factories.

San Pedro's relatively booming economy gave it the reputation for being the "industrial capital of Honduras." This attracted and still attracts—people from all over the country, especially rural Honduras, who come to San Pedro in search of more prosperous futures. Based on the 1988 Honduran national census, it was estimated that by 1992 San Pedro had an urban population of 361,938. The numbers working in the city and living in the surrounding areas of the Sula Valley raised the total metropolitan population to approximately 407,000 people (UIES 1993:27). By 1996 this had increased to 442,472. and, by 1999, 553,024 just for the city (Ciudad, DIEM/FNUAP, communication of December 1998), with an undetermined but higher number of people living in the now densely populated surrounding areas.

The most recent catastrophe to hit San Pedro, and Honduras in general, was hurricane and tropical storm Mitch. Hurricane Mitch itself did not enter continental Honduras, thanks to the coastal mountain range Nombre de Dios ("Name of God") that stopped the strong, category 5, winds. The problem was that hurricane Mitch became stationary over the Honduran Bay Islands and for almost an entire week Honduras was under constant tropical rain. This created a tropical storm which devastated continental Honduras. Between October 26 and 31, 1998, it rained almost non-stop. This flooded a great part of the country. Floods destroyed most bridges and severely damaged most roads. About 80 to 90per cent of Honduras' national crop production for the year was ruined (Honduras president Carlos Flores' communi-cation via a televised address, November 1998).

The local newspaper *La Prensa* of December 3, 1998 published offi-cial statistics a little more than a month after the catastrophe: 5,877 deaths with 1.4 million people directly affected (usually left homeless). These very large numbers are also huge **percentages** if we consider that the total estimated population of Honduras as of March 1998 was 5.7 million (García Trujillo, Paredes, and Sierra 1998:12). Mitch also brought disease: 66 cases of leptospirosis (a strange and dangerous dis-ease transmitted by rat and other animal urine), outbreaks of regular and hemorrhagic dengue, malaria, cholera, and dysentery.

Thus, it should not be surprising that the feelings of danger and vio-lence in which gender and sexual relations are embedded in San Pedro might be deeply rooted in the cultural and geographical memory of the region. After all, disease, natural disasters, and violence have been endemic to San Pedro for centuries.

3

THE WILL NOT TO KNOW

○ ○

"[There is] a traditional difference between that which people know and that which they agree to admit that they know, that which they see and that which they speak of."

------*Henry James*

Unmasculine males are labeled *locas* , *maricones, maricas*, (both derived from the female personal name María), *culeros* (someone whose anus is his essence) and other derogatory terms. It is presumed that their "nature" is to seek anal penetration. Conventionally masculine males, whatever their involvement in recurrent same-sex sex may be are generally not marked with special terms: they are just *hombres* (men). Adonis García, the Mexican sex worker narrator (who strays from *hombre* impenetrability) in Luis Zapata's novel expresses a widespread sentiment: *¿Por qué todos mis pinches actos deben tener un corolario de palabras, tan inútiles como gastadas?"*—Why must there be a corollary of useless, tired words for every little single act of mine? (1985[1979]:47). As Prieur (1998: 31) wrote, "When it comes to *jotas'* masculine-looking partners, the use of the words is even more difficult, since one of the characteristics of these men is that they do not designate themselves as anything else than men." This has made terminology that describes *hombres* and their homosexual practices scarce in non-homosexual circles, unlike the abundant (derogatory) popular terminology that exist for the "homosexual" (see Murray and Dynes

31

1995) or the elaborated *loca* taxonomy of kinds of *hombres* discussed later in this book.

The penetrability of the *locas* is inferred from their visible lack of masculinity. That the sexual conduct of masculine men is penetrative is similarly taken for granted: gender and sexuality are (unless or until proven otherwise) presumed to be consistent ("normal"/"natural"). Interest in seeking proof of such discrepancy is exceedingly rare in Latin American cultures, least of all on the part of homosexual males who are heavily invested in their partner's masculinity. Aside from his own fantasies about his own "real man" or "real men" in general, "those who are not competing for regard as machos generally have the sense not to rattle the fragile masculinity of those who present themselves as *machos*, knowing that the latter are all too likely to lash out at anyone who questions their (sacred , though often fragile) masculinity," as Murray (2000:271) put it. As Bourdieu (2001:51) wrote, "the impossible ideal of virility is the source of an immense vulnerability." More specifically, as Wikan (1984:646) wrote: "To be a man in a society where sanctions are discreetly expressed, if at all, and everyone is provided with a 'public' that in a sense 'honours' him, does not make life all that easy. The man must steer a deft and elegant course with very few signals from that public who are his judges. He can never be sure that his value is what he thinks it is, as he observes his bland reflection in his polite spectators." This indirectness also "insulates both the local and the overarching social system from direct challenge," as Murray (1997:16) noted after quoting Wikan's epitomization.

Culturally plausible deniability

The extent to which the taboo against speaking about sex in general and about the homosexuality of the *hombres* in particular account for the invisibility and even for the believed absence or nonexistence of homosexuality in the lives of these *hombres* who have sex with *homosexuals* is an important—though complex—matter. Analysts have to wonder whether *hombres* who have sex with effeminate men and later completely deny having done so, knowingly lie about this, or whether they really believe what they say.

The easy answer is "Both!" One can see why an *hombre*, living in a heterosexist and homonegative society want to deny that he has had sex with other males. What is more interesting, however, is when an *hombre* "lies" to himself about his homosexual behavior. The absence of *hombre* homosexuality in public discourse impedes him from putting it into words or thoughts, and encourages living in a state of denying, or at least not cognizing what he recurrently does. This, in turn, perpetuates the cultural model of penetrating men and penetrated males who fail in multiple ways to meet the standard of being a man.

Monique Wittig argued that language "is a set of acts, repeated over time, that produce reality-effects that are eventually misperceived as 'facts'" (in Butler 1990: 115). This repetition is what Derrida (1998:18) has called "citationality," because in order for an utterance to effectively signify a referent, the listener has to have become already acquainted with the referent and the signifying connection between it and the utterance. And this acquaintance is built through repetition or re-iteration of the utterance. Thus, each time an utterance is fulfilling its signifying role it is because of a citationality effect—the word has "cited" what was already inscribed in the mind of the receiver and reinforces such inscription. If there is not a word or signifier in the Lacanian Symbolic whose meaning or signifying connection to a referent was learned over repetition and imitation, then there is no perceived referent. At least in the realm of the Father or the Symbolic, a referent that has not been signified does not exist (Lacan 1977, 1978; Butler 1990, 1993). As Derrida (1988:13) claimed, "The performative does not have its referent...outside of itself or, in any event, before and in front of itself. It does not describe something that exists outside of language and prior to it. It produces or transforms a situation, it *effects*."

Prieur (1998:162-163) provided an example of a bisexual man playing a game of avoiding signification—whether he was in denial or not.

As long as the narratives about sexuality were kept at the strictest level of privacy, as long as the issue was not made public by speaking out about it, as long as his homosexuality was not signified, everything was fine—there was no homosexual referent. But when Marta made a public statement about them being transvestites, the spell vanished. Jorge was put in the difficult situation of either publicly acknowledging that he was dating another male, which could have implied a drastic change in his own identity and perception of self, or fleeing to keep his identity intact. Jorge chose to flee.

Murray (1996b:239) related what was for him a revelatory experience that he had in Guatemala in 1978 with a man he called "Raúl." Raúl told Murray that he was *activo*, i.e., one who is never penetrated. They had sex, during which Murray anally penetrated Raúl. Back on the street after sex, to Murray's shock, Raúl told Murray that he "didn't get fucked and never would."

Another narrative of a *pasivo* (insertee) *hombre* in denial was immortalized in the homosexual Cuban writer Reinaldo Arenas' autobiography:

> I remember once, getting off the bus, I approached a muscular adolescent. We didn't waste words. One of the advantages of a pickup in Cuba was that not much talk was needed. Things were settled with a look, asking for a cigarette or saying you lived nearby and would he like to come with you. If he accepted, everything else was understood. The young man accepted, and once inside my home, surprisingly asked me to play the role of the man. Actually that gave me pleasure too, and the man went down on me. I fucked him and he enjoyed it like a convict. Then, still naked, he asked me, "And if anybody catches us here, who is the man?" He meant who fucked whom. I replied, perhaps a little cruelly, "Obviously, I am the man, since I struck it into you." This enraged the young man, who was a judo expert, and he started to throw me against the low ceiling; thank God, he would catch me in his arms on the way down, but I was getting an awful beating. "Who? Who is the man here?" he repeated. And I, afraid to die on this one, replied, "You, because you are a judo expert." (1993:102-03)

I also witnessed a situation of blatant denial in San Pedro Sula during the fall of 1998. My friend Fausto, Fausto's friend Charlie, and I were having a drink in a centrally located shopping center, the Pasaje Valle. I noticed that a man, about 24 years old, was "cruising" us.[1] I alerted Fausto, who then invited the man to join us at the table. The man's name was Johnny. Fausto was not very subtle about his sexual intentions and offered to pay for a hotel room where all of us—included Johnny—could go and "relax." Johnny accepted. In the hotel Fausto fucked Johnny in a rather mechanical way and then got more passionately involved with Charlie, leaving Johnny aside.

I observed everything from close up, including the sexual acts. I noticed that Johnny was quietly weeping. I assumed that the reason why he was sobbing was because he felt used and objectified like a masturbatory hole by Fausto, who was now more interested in Charlie. I approached Johnny and we talked. Between tears he told me that this was his first homosexual experience. He confided to me that he has been in love with his best male friend for years, and he wished his first homosexual experience had been with his best friend instead of with Fausto. I then asked him if it hurt to be anally penetrated for the first time. He looked at me in a combination of astonishment and dismay.

---

1.   I have used the English slang verb "to cruise" as a translation for the Mexican/Central American Spanish slang verb "*ligar*," which means to go out to public spaces, such as streets and parks and exchange glances, gazes, and stares with other men or women with the purpose of initiating a sexual/romantic adventure. *Ligar* also implies to meet someone after the initial exchange of gazes. In mainstream Spanish, *ligar* means to tie up, to unite, even to glue things together. Taylor (1985) gives a different meaning and attributes a different origin to the word ligar: "Mexican homosexuals distinguish between anonymous encounters (*fichas*) and romantic encounters (*ligas*). These terms reflect social values, for a *ficha* is a poker chip given by a client to a prostitute for sexual services in a very cheap brothel, while *liga* comes from the verb *ligar*, meaning 'to alloy precious metals'" (p. 122). More than the preciousness of metals, it is their fusing together that makes *liga* a metaphor for making sexual connections. At least in Honduras, only *liga* is used for cruising and it denotes both a romantic and a quick sexual encounter.

What?!—he said. I have *never* been penetrated!—he almost screamed. I quickly changed the subject as I was afraid his astonishment would escalate into a nervous breakdown.

None of the *hombres* I interviewed ever acknowledged having been penetrated. Prieur faced a similar situation:

> All of the *mayates* [masculine males involved with transvestite ones] I interviewed answered that they were never penetrated. Yet again, on the basis of what their partners told me, I am inclined to believe that some of them were not telling the truth. The *jotas* had warned me that no *mayate* would ever admit to having been penetrated—because that is something that cannot be said. This is of course a methodological problem, but I believe it is also a finding, since I came to realize why they cannot admit it: to be passive means to be *homosexual*, and this in turn means not to be a man. It is therefore something that should not happen, and if it has happened, it should not become known. (1998:199)

They cannot admit having been penetrated **because** they are *hombres*: they are masculine, which then makes them culturally (and linguistically) impenetrable—both in their own minds and in the general view. According to Murray (1995:63), the actual anal penetration of an *hombre* is "ignored 'by the culture,' or, rather, by Latino males who don't want to know, talk about, or think that masculine appearances do not necessarily validate untainted masculine essence." More than a matter of personal denial, it is a matter of cultural feasibility: a "man" is *always* the one who penetrates. A man who is penetrated is a cultural impossibility, an oxymoron. "I never get fucked" then becomes more a statement about identity than about behavior (see Murray 1996a:255n23).

Only during the liminal and extraordinary moment of sexual intercourse may an *hombre* sometimes admits to enjoying being penetrated—at least while it is happening. However, immediately after ejaculation, cultural models take over again, as for Johnny. Fausto told me of a situation of an *hombre* admitting that he was enjoying being "possessed":

> INTERVIEWER: Was he always the one who penetrated you?
> FAUSTO: Yes, at the beginning, always at the beginning.
> I: How many times?
> F: I don't know how many times. Perhaps three or four times. Something like that.
> I: And then you "turned him over."
> F: (laughter) Afterwards it was **me** who took the active role.
> I: Was this his first experience of being penetrated?
> F: He was a virgin. That's why it hurt him. It hurt him **and** it hurt me. It was a difficult penetration, not as other men I've penetrated, where to put it in is so easy I get lost in them, I sink into them.... Only recently I've been able to penetrate him. More or less, and only once each time we meet, because the second time he can't take it, it is too sore.
> I: Have you ever been able to talk about this with him?
> F: It's something that's not discussed. It's not dealt with, really. I can joke about it, though. You know that I'm a big joker...it's only possible through jokes—through jokes to say a few things, nothing seriously. The only time we talk about this is precisely when we are making love. Then he speaks and say: "I surrender to you, my love," I'm yours," "I haven't belonged to anyone else," "Only to you I can—" He gives himself up and all that.

Whether Fausto's *hombre* lover was being truthful about his anal virginity is not the point. What is important here is that the *hombre* was able to verbalize that he was enjoying being possessed by Fausto. Fausto added later that he was positive that the *hombre* would kill him if he learns that Fausto had talked about this.

I had something of a similar experience of departure from an *hombre*'s public stance in an encounter that was less than completely private:

Visiting La Ceiba, Osvaldo and I had early dinner and then walked to the Parque Central. There, Osvaldo spotted a *buitre* he was looking for. (Osvaldo knew this *buitre* through Helvecio.) The young man smiled at Osvaldo, and we kept walking. The *buitre* was talking to some buddies and we didn't want to "burn" (*quemar*) his reputation.

We waited at the next corner of the Parque Central. After few minutes the *buitre* joined us. His name was Julio, and he had just turned 21 a few days before. He was nearly six-feet tall, slim, light-complexioned, and had curly hair. We told him that we were looking for a place to spend the night and he suggested Hotel Príncipe, close to the Parque Central.

Once at the hotel, we chose a L.150 (about US$11) room with two beds for the night. It was about 7: 00 PM when the three of us went to the room. After a while, the negotiation began. Julio wanted Osvaldo's belt (in exchange of sex, it was implied although not openly said). Osvaldo didn't want to give his belt away. After much negotiation, I proposed the following deal, which Julio accepted: Julio had to "satisfy" both of us, then escort us to a night club, spend some time at the club, and then escort us back to the hotel. In exchange, I would pay him L.100 (c. US$8) for all this "service," the approximate value of Osvaldo' belt.

Once Julio agreed to these terms, he took a shower and emerged naked. Osvaldo posed for him and Julio got an erection. I put a condom on Julio's 8-inch penis and briefly fellated him. Then Julio engaged in foreplay with Osvaldo. Then he wanted to penetrate Osvaldo "*armas al hombro*" (missionary position in which the bottom's legs rest on the top's shoulders), but Osvaldo didn't like that position. Then Julio lost the erection.

Julio returned to me and we engaged in foreplay in my bed. Julio got an erection again. He tried to penetrate me in missionary position, but he did it too roughly and I stopped him. Julio lost his erection again.

He went to play with Osvaldo, but he barely got an erection. Finally, he sat on Osvaldo's bed against the wall, with no condom, and while Osvaldo was kissing him in the mouth I masturbated Julio with one hand and with the other I played first with his testicles, then with his perineum until I reached his anus.

Julio seemed to be more aroused when I played with his anus than he had been in anything else he had done with either of us. This was a secret between him and me. Osvaldo stopped kissing and looked down, so he could have seen that I had my hand deep under Julio's thighs. I took my hand out to avoid embarrassing Julio.

Early on, I had asked Julio if I could touch his buttocks and he said "no." Well, now I was not only touching his buttocks, but I had my finger **inside** his anus and I was massaging his prostate. Julio also told us before, during the negotiation, that he wouldn't let the other watch while he was having sex with one of us. He also didn't want us to see him naked, or to have sex with the lights on. Nevertheless, we had the lights on, we watched him having sex with the other one, and he ran naked from one bed to the other, in varying stages of tumescence. Julio had not had dinner that day and had lost much weight in the preceding months after he had been kicked out of his home. I assumed that his difficulty in keeping an erection had more to do with his malnutrition than with the fact that he was having sex with other men (or was disgusted by that). He seemed quite comfortable with us; he would kiss in the mouth, fully hug and let himself be hugged. Also, Osvaldo claims that Julio is a "professional *buitre*" and that he has already been in stable, although short-lasting, relationships with at least four *locas*. One was in La Ceiba and three in San Pedro (with Helvecio, Pino, and Tony). Also, Julio didn't need alcohol to disinhibit him for sex with males.

Finally Julio reached orgasm as I was hugging him and playing inside his anus. He propelled a large volume of ejaculate as far as his shoulders. Then, around 9: 30 PM, we dressed up and went to the clubs. Julio was walking on the street in a extremely macho demeanor, spitting frequently—a marker of extreme masculinity and roughness. The clubs were empty and boring. After he dropped us at the hotel, he asked for his L.100. The deal was clear and Julio followed it to the letter. Then he rightfully claimed his payment.

The conspiracy of silence and homosexual indirect discoursing

Privacy is practically nonexistent for the lower classes of most Latin American cities. Extensive consanguinal and affinal kin and sometimes friends and other visitors inhabit the Latin American home at any time. It is not uncommon for several people to share the same bed at nighttime.

Although sexuality is a daily aspect of life, most everyone politely acts as if they "do not know." Endeavoring to live together without having their lives mixed ("juntos pero no revuletos"—together but not scrambled), a pair of brothers who shared the same room about whom Murray (1995:37) wrote, both had sex with males. Not only did they not discuss that with each other, both refused to speculate about the other's sex lives to the alien sex-partner of one of them. Similarly Joseph Carrier observed a situation of lack of privacy in Guadalajara, Mexico where the family acted as if nothing had happened:

> At its peak the party numbered about eighteen. There were no females present. Only Arturo and the other contestant were in drag. The party consisted of dancing, drinking, joking, a little conversation, and a lot of petting. The dancing took place both in the courtyard and in Fernando's room. Since the relatives had a full view of the little courtyard, the petting took place only in the room. Several couples were lying on Fernando's large bed embracing and kissing. Several couples were kissing as they danced. At one point in the evening I noticed Fernando's youngest brother standing at the foot of the bed watching the couples and fondling his genitals. Another time I saw his elder sister pass through the room to use the toilet in back. (1995:109)

A conspiracy of silence is required for *hombres* and their homosexually identified partners to meet and socialize in public spaces without offending public morals and trespassing established codes of morality. Both Annick Prieur (1998:187) and Clark Taylor (1978, 1985) noticed the careful discretion with which masculine men socialized with homosexually identified men in public settings in Mexico City, so discretely that only people who are *entendido*—"in the know," participants in the subculture—would notice attempts at connections being made. Manuel Arboleda G. (1995: 102-03) described similar discretion in Lima, Peru.

There are several ways in which people in the "*ambiente*" of male-male sexual connection interact with each other to avoid being noticed or labeled as homosexuals using specific "body idiom, sequence of positions, and verbal 'protective disclosure routines'" (Taylor 1985: 128, building on Goffman 1959). Verbal "protective disclosure routines" include specific ways of speaking and semantics only known by the people in the *ambiente.* If someone who does not belong to the *ambiente* is addressed with these words, he or she will simply not understand to what the interlocutor is referring to and, ideally for the people in the *ambiente*, the situation will not escalate beyond an apparently innocuous misunderstanding.

Murray (1980), Murray and Dynes (1995), Kulick (1998), and others have collected some of the local homosexual vocabulary in Latin American sexual cultures. I quickly observed that in the Honduran *ambiente*, the special homosexual lexicon was used by—and seemingly known to—only those who considered themselves homosexuals, not by the *hombres.* who penetrated one or more homosexual Honduran. As Arboleda found in Lima and Murray in Guatemala City a decade earlier than my fieldwork, the masculine insertors did not socialize (or cruise) together, while homosexuals socialized with each other and watched for solitary hunters for homosexual sexual partners. Except in the realms of the homosexuals' fantasy, desire, and myth, *hombres* played a marginal role in the Honduran homosexual *ambiente.* When they entered the *ambiente*, they tended to interact only one-on-one, usually with whomever was their homosexual partner at that moment. Self-acknowledging Honduran homosexuals on the other hand, tended to socialize with each other, learning and using a lexicon unknown to their *hombre* partners. used homosexual slang in those situations. *Hombres*, of course, also socialized with other *hombres*, but not as part of the *ambiente*, and certainly not on the basis of shared interest in homosexuals or homosexuality! When *hombres* found each other in a situation of social contact with the partners of other homosexuals, that is, when *hombres* found each other in the *ambiente*, they remained distant, even hostile, to each other.

The first time I formally interviewed Osvaldo in 1994, he shared with me some of his homosexual lexicon, some of which I had already come to know through informal conversation:

> INTERVIEWER: Now, speaking about special homosexual vocabulary, what would be the purpose of using it?
> OSVALDO: It is mainly used when two homosexual males find themselves surrounded by heterosexual people and they don't want their conversation to be understood because many times it might be personal stuff. This is when the jargon is used. This is one of the reasons why this jargon has been created in the homosexual *ambiente*. Another reason would be to avoid scandalizing the heterosexual population with words that if they are said like heterosexuals say them, they [the heterosexual population] would become alarmed. For example, relations of the "anal/oral kind." If people hear these words, not like I just said them, but like they are vulgarly used in our country, like "*mámame el culo*" [rim my ass], people would get very scandalized. For example, one can refer to male genitalia that most people call "*paloma*" or "*pija*" [equivalent to saying "dick" or "cock"] without mentioning those words.
> I: How can you refer to male genitalia without saying "*paloma*" or "*pija*"?
> O: For example, when I'm going with another gay friend on the

bus, or when we are walking in downtown San Pedro and we see a man with a fairly big crotch [we say]: "*¡Mirá el vos de vos de mi tío cómo lo tiene!*" [literally, "look at the you of you of my uncle, how he has it"].

I: And what words do you use for the different sizes of penises I have heard *locas* using several different words to refer to penis sizes.

O: *Cutís*, the smallest ones; *abicutis*, a little bit bigger; *omba-omba*, medium size; *cafú*, large; *extra-cafú*, extra-large.

I: And to have sex, [what words do you use]?

O: *Parchís* [fucking]. For example, when you are in a meeting of homosexuals, and you leave accompanied by a man, and later you come back, they will ask you "¿Ya parchaste?" [did you fuck?] or they will say "Ese hombre te quiere para parchar" [that man wants you for a fuck] or "Andate a parchís con él" [go and fuck with him].

I: Are there other words?

O: Homosexuals who use drugs use the word "*cotís*" instead of marijuana.

I: And heterosexuals don't recognize it?

O: No, even drug addicts who use marijuana don't recognize the word; only the people who use the homosexual slang do.[2]

According to Osvaldo special homosexual vocabulary is used to avoid offending public decency, and to keep illicit activities (including drug consumption) invisible.

In the case of masculine men, they look to escape being labeled as homosexual by preferring dates who are not too visibly "homosexual." Contrary to what the stereotype indicates, in my fieldwork in Honduras I found that masculine penetrators of homosexuals prefer their partners to appear at least passably masculine in public. For instance,

---

2. These terms were confirmed to me by other interviewees as well. The term *parchar*, however, seems to be of recent invention and Miguel, for one, did not use it.

Gerson Donali (in an section of our interview included in chapter 6), expressed relief that his partner does not look obviously effeminate, so that Gerson is not embarrassed to be seen with him, whereas being seen with a transvestite or a flamboyant homosexual "shooting off feathers" (the metaphor for making one's homosexuality obvious) does.

Gender nonconformity is understood as a public statement about homosexuality. Far from an innocuous homosexual act occurring in private, someone flaunting his homosexuality by being gender nonconforming is what really seems to amuse, shock or bother (depending on the context) people witnessing this. Public demonstration of gender nonconformity is poor manners, and regarded as an outrageous violation of public order and decency codes. Some regard it as taking the privacy of what one does in bed into the daylight streets—something so unbearable for some people, that they react with mockery or less verbal aggression against what they see as hostile, antisocial, aggressive conduct.

4

THE IDEOLOGY OF
GENDER EXOGAMY

o o o o o o o o o o o o o o o o o o o o o o o o o o o o o
"Genders, far from being simple 'roles' that can be played at
will, are inscribed in bodies, and in a universe from which
they derive their strength." (Bourdieu 2001:103)

I n the ideology both of homosexually identified Hondurans and of
the heterosexually identified men who penetrate them, the *hombre*
must only be a penetrator and must never show any desire toward the
maleness of the homosexual. That is, he must never kiss, fellate or
touch the genitalia of the homosexual. Doing so instantly destroys the
loca's fantasy. Someone who does such things can longer be viewed as a
real man (*un hombre completo*), and is not a suitable partner for the
homosexual.

The "natural[ized]" norms by which the homosexual
male has no penis and an *hombre* has no anus

"The dominated apply categories constructed from the point of
view of the dominant to the relations of domination, thus making
them appear as natural." (Bourdieu 2001:35)

There is a tacit agreement between *hombres* and homosexuals to
maintain this fantasy scenario of absolutely consistent, rigidly gendered

sexual conduct.[1] *Locas* act as if they have no penis (cannot penetrate) and *hombres* act as if they have no anus (cannot be penetrated). A passage from the interview with Horacio illustrates this commitment:

> INTERVIEWER: Do they [the *hombres*] play with your penis when...they have sex with you?
> HORACIO: No. No one has tried to do that. At least none of the persons with whom I have wanted to be emotionally involved [has]. They've never attempted to play these types of games, because if that were the case, I wouldn't have it, and I'd immediately dismiss them.
> I: Has that happened to you?
> H: Yes, it has happened to me, but not with the persons with whom I really wanted to stay, but with some of those with whom I have just wanted to have a moment of distraction.
> I: Even if you didn't know they were going to react like that, when they did, you didn't want to be with them again?
> H: Yeah: that's it [the end of any possibility of a partnership].
> ...
> HORACIO: He doesn't touch my penis because I wouldn't let him. Right?
> I: But some have wanted to touch it?
> H: No, no, no, no! If they want to, they are not my partners any longer.

Miguel provided a parallel explanation of why a *hombre* should never accept being touched in a form that implies he could be penetrated:

---

1.   See Murray (1987:196, 1995:52) on *maricón* fantasies of impenetrable, hypermasculine *hombres*. He, Carrier (1995), Prieur (1998), Schifter (1998), and others have noted behavioral variations from the ideal norms of a "natural" distinctiveness of kinds that are more ardently defended by the penetrated men than by those penetrating them.

INTERVIEWER: What do you do when you meet an *hombre*? What do you do sexually?

MIGUEL: Make love—one sucks them, one is fucked from behind, but one doesn't touch them, because they can't tolerate or accept it.

I: In what sense can't you touch them?

M: Their buttocks, you know?

I: They can't tolerate that?

M: No. Absolutely not. You can touch the penis, suck it, everything, but never introduce anything into him.

I: And can he touch your genitals?"

M: No, absolutely not. From the very moment he tries to touch there, I leave him.

"Proper" sexual behavior for the *hombre* is to grab the buttocks of the *loca*, possibly to suck the *loca*'s nipples, and to penetrate the *loca*'s mouth and anus. An *hombre* should not kiss the *loca* on the mouth, at least during the first months of the relationship.

The *hombre* must be "masculine" by the conventional cultural standards fetishized by *locas*, and he is usually younger than the *loca*. In most cases, the *hombre* is still a young, unmarried man, between the ages of 15 and 25. Murray (1995:50-51) contended that some anthropologists who provided an "anything goes" pictures "confuse the men with the boys. Specifically, homosexual experimentation is more acceptable among the unmarried young, but is increasingly threatening to masculine reputation with age…. There is an age limit, albeit a fuzzily bounded one. I would hazard that the age has been increasing along with the age of marriage."

Because the *loca* is usually older, the *loca* generally has more money than the *hombre*, although both the *loca* and the *hombre* tend to belong to the lower class. The *loca* financially supports or at least contributes to the support of the *hombre,* and sometimes provides financial assistance to the family of the *hombre* as well. The *hombre*'s family may accept his relationship with the *loca* but the issue is rarely or never discussed. There is what Murray (1997) characterized as a positive **will not to know** about such relationships involving offspring and siblings. The cultural prescription is not just "Don't ask" and "Don't tell," but "Don't even think about it!"

The *hombre* may at times be violent—physically and emotionally—to the *loca*, especially when he is drunk. The *hombre* may simultaneously maintain romantic and/or sexual relationships with women. He usually does not hide his heterosexual relationships from family and neighbors, as he does his homosexual relationship. He may, indeed, brag about his female conquests, especially in front of his male friends, and even in front of his *loca* partner. Although the *loca* may be jealous and afraid of being abandoned for a more "natural" (i.e., female) partner, assertions about such relationships also bolster the public masculinity of the partner, culturally "proving" that this is a "real man" (not least to rival *locas* who are eager to doubt that someone else has found and is in a relationship with someone completely man, an *hombre completo*).

Despite the often contemptuous and sometimes abusive treatment from the *hombre* who "gets off" into the orifices of the homosexual body, the *loca* usually pays for the *hombre*'s expenses and gives him spending money. Within the culture of machismo in which they live, *locas* choose to give up most[2] male privileges and to reproduce hierarchical structures of male domination in which *locas* pay to play the role of subordinated and oppressed women, even though one might imagine the possibility of their using their relatively greater economic resources to dominate their partners (out of bed). The script Prieur reported for transvestite Mexican homosexuals is the same:

---

2. The exception, the male privilege largely retained by effeminate males is mobility: ranging freely through the streets rather than being confined to the home. As will be discussed below, sometimes they cannot pass freely through public (male) space, but they have to get out and make money to support their short-term or long-term *hombre* partners or to provide them with tribute (i.e., "presents" that are necessary for a relationship to continue).

> They [*locas* or *jotas*] pay for themselves and often quite a bit for the
> other (the *hombre*), but while money in many contexts provides the
> right to demand something from the one who is paid for—such as
> services, or housework—the *jotas* have to (and want to) treat their
> lovers as men who are not given orders, and who do not do the
> dishes. Actually, out of their desire to be regarded as feminine, they
> prefer to do such work themselves. They get sex and they give sex,
> but while they may make a considerable effort to give the other
> pleasure, they cannot expect him to do the same. They probably do
> not want it to be otherwise, as they often do not want to remind
> their lover (or themselves) about their male sexual organs; they do
> not want them to be touched. (1998:242)

Once the *hombre* has become a fully grown man with some sort of
skill or profession, even if the homosexual has financed his studies, the
hombre leaves the homosexual, marries a female, and formed a new
household. Maybe, after a few years, the homosexual will find another
lover with whom to live. More likely, however, the homosexual will
spend many years between relationships, having, instead, only casual
sex. But the homosexual might also be too busy taking care of his ill
mother or raising the orphan child of his deceased, single-mother sister
to be thinking of romance. The homosexual may spend long hours as
well supervising the family's business or the beauty salon that he owns
in a central area of town.

This is (obviously) an idealization of what is supposed to be the
script, though it is normative in the statistical as well as the prescriptive
sense of "norm." The ideal model of what an *hombre* ought to be—and
is—regularly fed by homosexuals' fantasies about their ultra-masculine
partners. As Murray (1995:56) put it, "Those who have dropped out of
the machismo competition generally have the sense not to rattle the
fragile masculinity of the *hombre*, who is all too likely to lash out at
anyone who questions his (sacred) masculinity. Just as it takes a slave to
be a master, the *pasivo* invests, persuades, polishes, and maintains his
fantasy of the 'real man' (*hombre-hombre*)." I agree with Murray about
how the fragile masculinity of the *hombre* needs to be sustained. How-

ever, he neglected the extent to which there are penetrators (*hombres*) without penetratees, especially men without regular (or any) access to female orifices. One cannot be a master without having slaves, but there are young, unmarried Latin American males posing as female-ravishers whose (heterosexual) exploits are not based on their behavior in any real world. Arboleda (1995:104-05) wrote of one instance "who was 29 and self-employed, did not engage in heterosexual relationships and had little interaction with women. Despite the fact that his sexual activities were exclusively with men, he denied any homosexual imputation. For him, only [penetrated] *pasivos* are homosexual."

However, as Murray argued, "The imaginary undifferentiated phallic supremacy of the *hombre*—supposedly common to Mediterranean cultures and to former Iberian colonies in the New World is too neat. Certainly, there are individuals who impersonate these ideal [strictly dichotomized] roles" (1995:52). Behaviorally, it may not be rare for things that are proscribed to occur in private: the *hombre* being penetrated by the homosexual, for example. Fausto, for instance, identifies himself as a *loca*, but anally penetrates most *hombres* he encounters, although it takes him a while to get to do this, he reports. Payment is necessary only at the beginning. Being penetrated by *hombres* also is necessary at the beginning, according to Fausto. He added: "if you get to kiss or touch [an *hombre*] on the back that means that [he] will let you penetrate him." In this context, being kissed (or touched) on the back as interpreted to indicate future anal receptivity.

The distinction between public and private discourses is important in this regard. For those involved, it is extremely important that at the level of public conception (the reference group being primarily other homosexuals), the *hombre* is the one who penetrates the homosexual. In this sexual culture, being an *hombre* implies being masculine and a penetrator. It is part of the essence of being an *hombre* within the *ambiente*. Complementarily, the homosexual embodies culturally expected female attributes such as sexual passivity and public deference to the dominating masculine partner. Statistical variation from the ideal norms is not reported outside homosexual circles, and may not even be cognized by those whose behavior varies from the ideal norms (though *locas* brag about their rival *locas' hombres* being penetrated, they insist on the impenetrability of their own partner).[3]

The sexually versatile masculine gay man has no place or even the possibility of one in more traditional Latin American conceptions in which masculinity and penetrativity are not distinguished. As Cáceres and Jiménez 1999:182-83) wrote of the traditional model as they elicited it from park hustlers in Lima, Peru, "a man cannot desire another man as a man, yet he could want to penetrate him as a male. Similarly, it is impossible for two men to have sex together: necessarily one of them, the one who crossed the boundaries in order to make sex possible, loses his status as a man." "Simply stated, there are men and then there are those who are fucked or get fucked by men," Morales (1997) wrote. Schifter and Aggleton (1999:143) also stressed that for Costa Rican male sex workers, the homosexual is the one who **shows** desire for other men: "When a preference for a special client is felt, the desire is usually repressed…. None claimed to feel sexual attraction towards a man, even during their childhood. All of them had their first sexual experiences with women, and enjoy sexual relationships with them, not with other men" (145, 144). Moreover, they prefer older men who, having lost their youthful good looks, are accustomed to paying: "Sex

---

3. Some of the accounts of *hombres* being penetrated by *locas* should be considered part of the corrosive (of pretensions to masculinity) ideology of the *jotas* and *locas*. In bragging about their conquests of other *jotas'* supposedly entirely phallic partners, they dismissed each of the other's partners as being, under a masculinist mask, also homosexual:

   Then Fifi and Gloria entered a contest. Which of them had sex with real men, and which of them had sex only with other *homosexuales*? With a seemingly perfect overview, they pattered out all the other's partners and always found a reason to label the poor guy a *homosexual*, claiming to always know of somebody who has penetrated him, or referring to the fact that the man in question has never been seen with a woman. The other *jotas* joined in, giving their opinion on the different men mentioned. (Prieur 1998: 169)

workers feel that by having sex with men of their own age they are 'homosexualizing' themselves" (146).

There are and have been (behavioral/statistical) divergences from the ideal norm of division into two distinct kinds of persons. Carrier (1976:120-21) long ago noted (with data from Guadalajara, Mexico) that, while "there is a low probability that both active and passive anal intercourse are practiced by both participants in a given homosexual encounter,…a little over forty percent of those playing the anal passive sex role and close to one-fourth of those playing the anal active sex role during their first sustained year, over time, incorporated the other sex role into their sexual repertoire." Also see the evidence of behavioral versatility from Mexico and Peru reviewed in Murray (1995:145-49). Moreover, a closer look at native sexual categories (primarily elaborated and used by *locas*) shows that there is a dynamic (over-time) continuum running between the ideal *hombre* and the ideal *loca*, as will be discussed below.

Before turning to the more elaborate distinctions among kinds of sexual actors which *locas* make, another forbidden, officially inconceivable kind of pairing must be considered.

Homosexuals don't like *tortillas*

When Helvecio claims that he does not like "to make tortillas," this does not mean that he does not like to cook or eat them. The metaphor in homosexual speech "to make tortillas" means the sex that takes place between two non-penetrating partners, that is, sex between two insertees, whether women or homosexuals (*pasivos*). Without the possibly of penile penetration being conceived, it is assumed that the only other possible sexual contact is to rub against each other, as when kneading, handling, and massaging the dough together to make tortillas; hence the metaphor "to make tortillas" for sex that does not include a man.[4]

---

4.   This metaphor is used across an extensive geographical range: see Murray and Dynes 1995:190; Kulick 1998b; Gaudio 1998.

Helvecio swore that in his fifty years on earth he had never "made a tortilla" with another homosexual. Sex between two homosexuals is not merely taboo, but inconceivable to him.

In the dichotomous gender economy of machismo fervently upheld by homosexuals, this taboo is applicable to two masculine men having sex, though there is not the "What can they use/do?" mystery. In Mexico Prieur heard "*jotas* comment with disgust at the sight of two mustache-wearing men kissing each other, seeing it as something 'abnormal'" (1998: 149). In Honduras I have heard of homosexuals being scandalized by gay masculine men being interested sexually in each other. U.S.-trained sociologist L. Cárcamo told me (during my first visit to Honduras in 1994) how he fruitlessly tried to create a support group for homosexuals to improve their self-esteem and develop what Cárcamo thought was a positive gay identity. He recalled a gathering which proved to be the last and definitive failure of this project: a party for homosexuals only. At this party, to Cárcamo's dismay, homosexuals who both looked too masculine or who both looked too feminine refused to dance together. Two homosexuals could dance together only if one of them looked masculine or was dressing as a man and the other looked feminine or was dressing as a woman. Cárcamo himself, who both looks masculine and dresses as a man, danced at that party with his younger boyfriend, who also looked masculine and was dressed as a man. The scandal was such that Cárcamo lost face and never managed to get the group together again after that.

Osvaldo's answers also reflect the normativity of gender in male-male relations when it comes to dance partners:

INTERVIEWER: Do you like to dress in women's clothes?
OSVALDO: Mmm, to a certain extent, yes. I feel some freedom that I don't have if I dress in men's clothes. For example, to dance with an *hombre* without being criticized.
I: So if you are dressed as a woman you can dance with an *hombre*—
O: Yes, if you are dressed as a woman and you dance with another

gay who is dressed in men's clothes, you are not criticized. But if you are dressed as a man and the other gay also is dressed as a man you are quite criticized within the gay community.

I: So when you dress in women's clothes you feel more free.

O: Yes, I feel more free. I can even walk on the streets with another male and no one criticizes me, because it is supposedly a woman and a man walking together.

Talking about activities at the legendary bar "El Gay," Miguel also confirmed the normativity of gender-distinct dance roles. For Miguel, however, more than how the homosexual was dressed, what mattered was if an *hombre* and a *loca* constituted the dancing couple:

INTERVIEWER: Did *hombres* dance with other *hombres*?

MIGUEL: *Hombre* with *hombre*, no.

I: What about *loca* and *loca*?

M: *Loca* with *loca*, yes.

I: On the dance floor, when everyone was dancing?

M: When everyone was dancing, no, but for the show, yes. To do their number.

I: And could a *loca* dressed as a man dance with a *loca-travesti*?

M: No. An *hombre* with a *loca*, yes. An *hombre* with a *loca-travesti*, or an *hombre* with a *loca* dressed formally.

In sum, neither an *hombre* nor a fellow *loca* should touch or have any interest in the genitals of a *loca*.

As Bourdieu (2001:40) wrote:

It has to be acknowledged both that the 'submissive' dispositions [*habitus*] that are sometimes used to 'blame the victim' are the products of the objective structures, and also that these structures only derive their efficacy from the dispositions which they trigger and which help to reproduce them…. The foundations of symbolic violence lies not in mystified consciousness that only needs to be enlightened but in dispositions attuned to the structure of domination of which they are the product.

What is conscious, what is reported to ethnographers or other kinds of interviewers to explain somatized social relationships is a set of standardized (normative) dispositions that have come to feel (to those playing complementary roles) "natural." Bourdieu recurrently evokes *amor fati* to characterize this—in the sense of a "love of destiny, the bodily inclination to realize an identity that has been constituted as a social essence and so transformed into a destiny" (50). Submission and withdrawal from phallic (self-)assertion are part of what American social scientists would call "role commitment" to the *pasivo*/homosexual/*loca* role, and Bourdieu calls "vocation" (for self-abegnation).

The vocation or role commitment of their *hombre* sexual partners is **not** to a role within same-sex sexual encounters, but to being masculine and penetrating even when in intimate contact with the body of a male (which is not conceived of as the body of a **man**, or, usually, even that of a potential man). Having sexual relations or ongoing love relationships with their "own kind" is not an alternative way they can conceive, and the *locas* most invested in the vocation of being penetrated find suggestions of reciprocity repugnant. As we shall see, the *hombres* also find suggestions of reciprocity uncomfortable, fearing that they might enjoy penetration and, thus, themselves have to become abjected homosexuals.[5]

Locas do not want their partners to become too involved in the homosexual *ambiente*, where other *locas* might attempt to steal them. Also—in their view even more tragic,—if *hombres* got too involved in the *ambiente*, they may lose part of their *hombria* and become more of

---

5.   They do **notice** the pleasure their penetrated homosexual partner has and may wonder what it feels like. Osvaldo, in my first interview of him, said that *hombres* see how much homosexuals enjoy being penetrated and grow increasingly curious about the mysterious pleasure of being penetrated, so that eventually they ask their homosexual partner to penetrate them to see if it feels as good as it seems to. This destroys the *loca* fantasy of the masculinity of the man. At the moment of that request, many *locas*, like Miguel Lemus, become completely disappointed in their *hombres*, whom they cease to conceive as *hombres* thereafter.

a *loca* and eventually even get penetrated and become competitors for the "real men" (*hombres completos*).

5

THE LOCA VIEW OF KINDS OF MALE SEXUAL ACTORS

L*ocas* actively reproduce their status as "oppressed," woman-like creatures as part of an ideology in which they emulate some attributes of women to attract "real" men into their sexual and romantic lives. Homosexuals want to believe that their own prized *hombre* really prefers women, and it is only because of the individual homosexual's special charm, unique seductiveness, and careful attention toward his lover that has waylaid the man into falling in love with one (and **only** one) homosexual.

However, this chapter shows that not only individual behavior but also the native categorizations of sexuality in Honduras are more complex than the heterosexual/ homosexual binary division or that of *hombres* and *loca*.[1] As Eve Kosofsky Sedgwick argued, there is a space between "gay" and "straight," which is broader and more complex than heterosexist regimes have made us believe. For Latin America, Murray (1987, 1995) has long argued that the rigid dichotomous division between *pasivo* and *activo* is more a shared fantasy than a reflection of actual behaviors. The categories shape as much as they reflect behavior. They are not just abstract cognitive structures but concepts that predict

---

1. For a detailed analysis of homosexual categorization in a lower-class Mexico City suburb, Ciudad Nezahualcóyotl, see Prieur (1998:24-31). Also see the extensive Spanish homosexual lexicon in Murray and Dynes 1995.

what can be done sexually, what a potential sex partner will expect and what he might allow to a partner whom he trusts. ("Trust" emerges as a leitmotif in *hombres'* accounts of relationships with homosexual partners, as is documented in the next chapter.)

Hombres

In the typology of *hombres*, most fully elaborated by those most interested in the category (dedicated *locas*), there are several subtypes. As Carioca told me:

> When the *hombre* begins having sexual relations with a homosexual and the *hombre* is new to the circle, he receives the name of *buitre* [generic term for vulture]. He begins to taste homosexuals' flesh, to nurture himself with it. As time passes, he receives another title: "*zopilote*" [turkey vulture]. Now, he not only has sexual relations with the first homosexual he met and with whom he was a partner, but he also begins to have sexual relations with other homosexuals as well. He has found that he likes homosexual relations so much that it doesn't matter to him anymore if he has sex with his first partner or with someone else.
>
> Still more "advanced" than the *zopilote* is the *cóndor* [the largest carrion-eating bird], who is the *hombre* who depends on the homosexual. [The *cóndor*] doesn't work anymore; he spends the 24 hours of the day with the homosexual. He has sex with the homosexual, and the homosexual maintains him. In the case of the *buitre*, it could be either that the homosexual pays him or does not. But in the case of the *zopilote* and *cóndor,* payment by the homosexual to the *hombre* is an essential feature of the relationship.

In September 1997, I was looking at a handsome young man from my bedroom window in the beach town of Tela. The man was dressing and undressing on the balcony of the next house. Osvaldo looked at him and dismissed him in a second. "He is *cuadrado*," Osvaldo said with a touch of disdain. I asked Osvaldo what that meant, and he responded that *cuadrado* (literally, squared) are *hombres* who are not in the *ambiente*, i.e., *hombres* who do not want to "play" with other men.

A year later, I asked Osvaldo the same question, but followed it up with questions about different categories for *hombres*.

> INTERVIEWER: How would you define a *cuadrado*?
> OSVALDO: Well, a *cuadrado* is a heterosexual person who is supposed to not have…sexual contact with [someone of] his same sex.
> I: How would you define a *buitre*?
> O: A *buitre* [literally, "vulture"] is a person who is like a [masculine] male prostitute, who sells his sex for money or goods, food, clothes, or any other object that might serve as a gift.
> I: Does the *buitre* have sexual relations with people of his same sex?
> O: Yes, he has sexual relations with people of his same sex.
> I: Are all *hombres* in the *ambiente buitres*?
> O: No, there are some who are not *buitres*. People call men who have who have sexual relations with homosexuals *parchís*. They are called *parchís* or *maridos* [literally, husbands], because the homosexual takes the woman's role…
> I: Are there *maridos* who are *buitres*?
> O: No, because this is something permanent. It's a constant and stable relationship between the homosexual and that *hombre*.
> I: But if the *marido* takes economic advantage of the homosexual, is he still not a *buitre*?
> O: No, he isn't a *buitre* anymore, because they live together on a daily basis; they might even rent an apartment together. Sometimes they share expenses, sometimes they don't. And the homosexual ends up [paying for everything]. It depends on the circumstances.
> I: Can there be a *parchís* who is also a *buitre* of the person who considers him a *parchís*?
> O: Yes, it can happen…
> I: How so?

O: Not everything is rigid. There are combinations of things. (1998 Interview)

There are *hombres* and **hombres**. The need to use the reinforcing construct *hombre completo* ("completely man") or (more rarely) *hombre-hombre* is not an accident and has to do with the fact that "*hombre*" has two different meanings, one that denotes biological sex and another that refers to gender. *Hombre* is the "male," as in a body that includes a penis, and also the "man," as in a grown up male who embodies and fulfills the gender expectations for a man in that society, including using the penis as a phallus (i.e., penetrating).

In the kind of context in which complete category sets are required (such as interviews by inquisitive foreign anthropologists). to indicate that someone is not only male but also a man, sometimes it is said that he is an *hombre completo* or *hombre-hombre*, a manly male. This is why in Figure 1 I have used "male, man" to refer to the *loca* category and "male, non-man," to refer to the *loca* category *loca*, who also happens to be an "*hombre*" but only at the level of sexual morphology, not gendered appearance and comportment (Fernández-Alemany 1996). Kulick (1998) also concluded that *travestis* were a sort of male non-men in Brazilian sexual cultures. Throughout this book every time I use the qualifying "*hombre*" I am referring to the masculine gender presentation rather than to biological maleness.

Tracas

Traca is an extremely complicated category, at the place on the continuum where the division between *hombre* and *loca* becomes more urgent. *Traca* seems to be the most fluid category of all; sometimes it seems to be a category for confusion and based in contradiction. In 1994 I heard the role-label *traca* for the first time, when I interviewed Miguel Ángel Lemus, from el Corcel Negro. Miguel was explaining to me what things his sexual partner would do and what things his sexual partner would never do with him:

INTERVIEWER: Is there a name for the man who touches your genitals?

MIGUEL: The man who touches my front area? We call him *traca*. Because they want to turn over. They want us to make love to them too…They are *tracas*, because they like to take and be taken…

I: Do the *tracas* have women as well?

M: Yes, they have women **and** they like to be homosexual.

…

I: Where does the word *traca* come from?

M: [From] the man who turns over, also called "pla-pla."

In 1998 I asked Osvaldo about the *traca*:

INTERVIEWER: How would you define a *traca*?

OSVALDO: A *traca* is what "biologically" would be defined as a bisexual; he can have sex with women as well as with men.

I: Oh, but *cuadrados, buitres, parchís,* and *maridos*: they all have sex with women, don't they?

O: No, they almost never do; there is an exclusivity, not to 100 per cent, but maybe to the 80 per cent, [to being] only with the homosexual; because some homosexuals are very possessive, so then there is some exclusivity.[2]

…

Traca means to be penetrated, either by a *loca* or by a *buitre*; and he also can penetrate a woman.

I: Like a *bisexual.*

O: Exactly. This is what it is. The only thing is that in our culture we call him *traca* so people out of the *ambiente* will not understand if they hear the word.

---

2. One *hombre* I interviewed had been almost killed by three *locas* who were his lovers and found out that he was cheating on them by also dating the other. Instead of attacking each other, the jealous and outraged *locas* attacked the man each thought was only sexual with himself.

I: What is the difference between a *traca* and another *hombre* who is not a *traca* but who does have sex with other men?

O: Well, that the other *hombre* does not have receptive sex; this is, he is not penetrated. And the *traca* is [penetrated].

...

I: Then, the difference between a *traca* and a *buitre* is that the *traca* has [sex with] more women, he is more bisexual than the *buitre* and the *buitre* is more exclusively involved with men. But later you told me that a difference was that the *traca* is penetrated by *hombres* and the *buitre* is not.

O: Look, the *buitre* is not penetrated. The *traca* is.

I: So that's the difference?

O: That would be one difference. Another one is that the *traca*, because of societal pressures, has to get married to a woman.

I: And what about the *buitre, marido,* and the like?

O: Those no.

I: They don't get married?

O: They do get married eventually, later on, but the *traca* does it because of societal pressures, although he is aware of his homosexuality, unlike the *buitre*, who doesn't think of himself as homosexual.

I: Why]is the *traca* considered homosexual?

O: Because he is receptive. Because he is penetrated. Had he not been penetrated, he wouldn't be considered homosexual.

I: Don't you think that they *{tracas]* might be *bisexuals* who get married because they really want to, or do you [still] think they are closeted homosexuals and that's the reason why they get married?

O: Well...

I: Or maybe both cases?

O: There are both cases, but the cases I have seen are mostly those ones.

I: Which ones?

O: Where the homosexual gets married because of family, work, or societal pressures.

The origin of the term *traca, pla-pla,* or *traca-traca* (the last elicited from Mango), probably comes from *trueque,* which means to barter or exchange items for an equivalent value, in this case, the exchange of anuses for penetration or of semen. There is a similar term for sexual versatility, or exchange of roles in bed in Brazilian Portuguese, *troca-troca*: "The space of sexual exploration is almost institutionalized through the culturally recognized game of *troca-troca* (literally, exchange-exchange), in which two (or more) boys take turns, each inserting the penis in their partner's anus" (Parker 1999:33).

Locas

Loca is a complicated category and criteria for defining a *loca* vary from person to person. Some say that *locas* are only the overtly effeminate homosexuals, like *obvios* and *travestis.* This is usually the definition of *loca* used by those who reject being labeled *loca.* Those who **accept** the label are eager to apply it to others, particularly others with pretensions of masculinity, saying that everyone who likes to be penetrated is a *loca. Loca* is a close translation for "homosexual" both in Honduran culture and in most of Iberoamerica, along with *maricón* and *marica. Marica* and *mariquita* also denote a weak and soft male—"sissy" is the best approximation in English.[3] In Honduras, the best translation for *mariquita* is *culero.* The term *culero obvio*usly comes from *culo,* anus.

---

3.   Murray (1995:62-63) recounts a discussion between two macho-self-identified East Oakland Chicanos about whether *maricón* in their dialect meant "timid" or sexually "penetrable": One maintained that "a *maricón* isn't necessarily homosexual. It's someone who can't take care of himself." However, this distinction from sexual expectations survived only for a moment. Then one of his friends completed the cultural syllogism immediately: "And therefore gets fucked." Murray asked, "You mean he gets 'fucked over'?" The second Chicano speaker answered, "Sure he does, **and** he takes it up the ass." The first speaker then agreed with this reformulation.

Although I first referred to it as someone who likes to "take it up the ass," (Fernández-Alemany 1997c), I now see the origin of *culero* in some very common expressions of fear in Latin America. They refer to the anus' contractions that sometimes occur in moments of fear. Thus, a male who is fearful and whom for that reason "se le hace el culo" [his ass shakes/contracts] is a *culero*, a sissy. Because fear and cowardliness signals lack of masculinity in the Honduran gender system studied, *culero*, like *mariquita*, is also a term used to denote homosexuality.

One *hombre* who understand *culero* only in the sense of timidity is Enrique:

> INTERVIEWER: What does the word *culero* mean?
> ENRIQUE: *Culero* , I imagine, must mean that you are afraid of someone else—
> I: Fearful?
> E: Yes, someone who is timid, who is afraid of darkness or who is afraid of someone taller than him—
> I: Doesn't it have anything to do with homosexual or with someone who has sex with homosexuals?
> E: No, not for me.

There is considerable variance in understanding of the term, however. Jaime, another *hombre* sees it as being applicable to those who like to penetrate anuses, what might be termed an "ass man" in English (without any tangible sense of being afraid to penetrate vaginas, since Jaime defines the *culero* as an *hombre*).

The literal meaning of the word *loca*, "crazy," is that a *loca* is someone who is not serious (Carrier 1995:104-06), the someone being feminine in grammatical gender. A male who is insufficiently serious enough to be an *hombre* is a *loca*. While an *hombre* is the one who is in command and can take responsibility of (and control and penetrate) others, the *loca* cannot. The *loca* is subject of mockery and contempt, a socially unfit and inferior being—a male not able to protect a masculine self from sexual use by real men, and, more scandalously, one who does not **want** to do so.[4] *Locas* are also equated to women of "easy virtue" (and, therefore, relatively easily penetrated), who are not taken seriously by *hombres* as potential wives and mothers of their legitimate children, but who provide welcome sexual outlets during leisure time outside the serious domain of augmenting and perpetuating the patriline. Because *obvios* and *travestis* are the most visible and easily recognizable *locas*, *obvios* and *travestis* are also the most marginalized group in society. They are the ones who suffer the most street scorn and violence. *Tracas* and *solapas*, on the other hand, are only stigmatized as *locas* by those who are more "in-the-know" (*entendido*). *Tracas* and *solapas* are marginalized little or not at all, although many suffer to a great extent because of their exhausting and paranoid efforts to maintain complete secrecy about their double lives.

Apparently, some *solapas* "outgrow" (or devolve from) an earlier stage of sexual freedom to a stage where they get married to women and become sexually more constrained (and perverse): they become *tracas*. Some *solapas* later in life become *obvios* and vice versa. Some *obvios* become *travestis* and some *travestis* become *obvios*. *Tracas* might turn out to be more *locas* even than *obvios* themselves and some *tracas* might even cross-dress.

There is even gossip that some *buitres* want to be (or have been) penetrated. I met three *locas* who began their "careers" in the *ambiente* as *buitres*. One is Fausto, who when he was an adolescent was the *buitre* of several older *locas* in San Pedro. Another one is Charlie, Fausto's friend, who at the time of my fieldwork considered himself a "gay activo." The third one lives in New York and considers himself *gay*.

Asking Osvaldo's attempt to explain the categories showed that they cannot be neatly lined up in sealed containers of attributes. At times, they seem to overlap and bleed from one category into adjacent ones in (multidimensional) cognitive space:

---

4.   For more about *locas'* lack of "seriousness" and how they utilize this to empower themselves, see "Causing un escándalo" in Chapter 8.

INTERVIEWER: What is a *solapa*?[5]

OSVALDO: A *solapa* is a homosexual, but as its name implies, a homosexual who is not *obvious*, that you can't tell just by seeing him.... The *solapa* is a homosexual who is aware of his homosexuality and who also is single, then he is not as pressured as the *traca*. The *traca* is an adult, unlike the *solapa*, who is a young man who feels less impeded to carry on a free lifestyle, who is not as...perverted as the *traca*'s is—

I: How?

O: Like, there are *tracas* who are sadomasochists and others who are voyeurs, fetishists, while the *solapa* is none of those, perhaps because he can live his sexuality more freely.

I: And how do you know that *tracas* do these things and *solapas* don't?

O: Because of my own experience and because of what some friends of mine in the *ambiente* have told me.

I: In what environments do the *traca* and the *solapa* have sex?

O: Well, the *traca* usually has sex with transvestites, with street commercial sex workers, unlike *solapas* who do it in a healthier environment.

I: Among *solapas*?

O: Among *solapas* and among gay *obvios*.

I: So that would be a difference between *traca* and *solapa*, but is there anything else? Is every *solapa* going to marry women? Are there some who don't get married?

O: Uhm, **most** don't get married. This is, because they are aware of their homosexuality, some of them have even told their families. Their families don't accept but tolerate them.

---

5.   The term *solapa*, literally "collar," comes from *asolapado*, which means collar-covered, like when someone raises the collar or *solapa* of his/her coat to cover the neck and sometimes part of the face, hiding from the cold but also from gazes of others.

Solapas sometimes get romantically involved with an *hombre*, but most of their relationships are of the "gay" type and with other *solapas*.

I: So both *tracas* and *buitres* are bisexuals but the *solapa* isn't.

O: The *solapa* isn't considered a *bisexual*, because he has only had sex with people of his same sex.

I: Therefore from the *solapa* and on [to the right, in Table 1] the categories are for 100 per cent homosexual...or is it *traca* homosexual as well?

O: Sometimes the *solapa* has to have a relationship with a woman. Especially if he is **very** *solapa*, he does it to continue maintaining a discreet silence around his homosexuality, because he's still not very aware of it.

I: What is then the difference between a *solapa* and a *traca*? Is it the same or are there differences to you?

O: Yes, I think there are differences. To begin with, the *solapa* is younger, more immature and at the same time he's more aware about his homosexuality; he can live his sexuality in a freer way, not under pressures, as the *traca* does.

I: And who is the *obvio*?

O: (laughs) [I think Osvaldo laughs here, because this is his own category.]

The *obvio* is the person, the homosexual who has mannerisms or is effeminate.[6] Regardless if he wants to or not, his femininity—rather his effeminacy—is noticeable.

I: Is there another difference between *obvio* and *solapa*?

O: Yes, the *obvio* tends to use clothes that are considered more feminine, women's outfits, pants, blouse, even some shoes that are unisex.

I: And the *travesti*?[7]

---

6.   The (obvious) cognate of *obvio* in English is "obvious," something that can be clearly seen and is readily evident. In this case, the homosexuality of *obvios* is evident at the first sight because of their effeminacy.

O: Well, the *travesti* (transvestite), as his name indicates, spends most of his time dressed as a woman. In our country, most *travestis* crossdress because he's a commercial sex worker; he lives off this image, and dresses as a woman most of the night and sleeps during the day.

I: And what does the *obvio* do for work?

O: Well, an *obvio* may work cleaning offices. If he has the privilege to study, he may work in a profession, although it will be very unlikely that he will be hired.

I: What type of jobs do the *obvios* whom you know of do?

O: Most of them do women's jobs. They are fashion designers, hairdressers, maids, and baby-sitters.

I: What about *travestis*? Is there anything else they do besides prostitution?

O: No. Most of them are prostitutes. There are no other possibilities for them. Maybe in other countries there are other possibilities for transvestites, but in Honduras they can only be whores.

This statement, although shocking, struck me as true, since I never met or heard of a full-time transvestite in Honduras who could work doing anything but street prostitution. This reality contrasts with other countries of Latin America such as Mexico (see Prieur 1998) and Brazil (see Kulick 1998) where transvestites can do other work such as being hairdressers, although the range is very limited. In Tegucigalpa I met a Salvadoran transvestite who had a mixed career: at night he did commercial sex work and during the day he taught dance in a school he had founded. But this took place in El Salvador and not in Honduras. Dur-

---

7.   Most of Prieur's (1998) and Kulick's (1998) work was done with transvestites. My work focused on the relation *hombre/loca,* which usually takes place between an *hombre* and a *loca,* the latter of whom is an *obvio* or a *travesti.* Of the fifteen homosexually identified males I interviewed, one more or less was a *travesti,* eleven more or less were *obvios,* and three more or less were *solapas.* Besides the *travesti* (Cindy), only five (less than half of *obvios*) admitted to having cross-dressed in the past, usually doing some prostitution on the streets as well.

ing the time he lived in Honduras he worked exclusively as a sex worker until the day a homophobic client shot him in the thorax, abdomen and legs. After a difficult and long convalescence period in a Tegucigalpa hospital, he returned to El Salvador.

Another alternative that is emerging for a few transvestites in Honduras is to work at one of the newly formed AIDS/gay organizations. But there are a very few vacancies available and the jobs require a level of literacy that many transvestites do not possess. Even worse, these organizations maintain an ambivalent attitude toward transvestites. On one hand, the organizations encourage transvestites to leave street prostitution because of its many dangers and low social status. On the other, and based on the ideals of North American gay models, the organizations reject transvestites and give them subtle (and at times not very subtle) messages that if transvestites really want to be part of the organization they must stop cross-dressing and adopt a more masculine look and behavior. The broader context in which marginalization of the transgendered people from the new gay organizations in Latin America takes place is analyzed in Chapter 9.

> I: What is a *"loca de closet"* [homosexual of the closet]?
> O: Oh, the *loca de closet* is the *solapa*.
> I: Is it the same?
> O: Yes, it's the same.
> I: And the *traca*?
> O: No, the *traca* isn't *de closet*, although somewhat he is. Because even though they are not aware of their homosexuality, I would consider them *de closet*.
> I: But it's more fuzzy. Less clear.
> O: Uh-huh.
> …
> I: Who are the *locas*?
> O: Well, the *locas* are the *travestis* and *obvios*.
> I: And the *solapas*?
> O: No, *solapas* are not considered *locas*, because they are not doing

crazy, flamey things around (*loqueando*).

I: And the *tracas*?

O: Even less, even though some *tracas* are quite *loca*. (laughter)

I: More than *solapas*?

O: Yes—I know some who are engineers and go out at night dressed as women and hang out with transvestites, ask to them for sex, ask the transvestites to penetrate them, things like that.

I: And wouldn't a *solapa* do that?

O: No.

I: So in a scale that goes from *cuadrado* to *travesti*, *traca* and *solapa* are in the right order, or should they go in a different order? [Looking at a preliminary version of what is Table 1 in this chapter.]

O: I think they are in the right order the way it is.

I: Even though there are *tracas* who are more of a *loca* than *solapas*?

O: Uhm, yes. But as *tracas* [they] always try to maintain their position...

...

I: Who are "*hombres*"?

O: Well, we are all *hombres* [natally male]. But for most people in *ambiente hombres* are the ones who have sex only with women.

I: So then is the *traca* an *hombre* or not?

O: Tracas are not considered *hombres* in the *ambiente*...

I: This is, they are considered *traca*.

O: Yes, *traca*.

I: And *loca*?

O: If the *solapa* isn't considered an *hombre*, even less the *obvio* is. Because they have a greater tendency to the feminine they aren't considered *hombres*.

I: So the *traca* isn't an *hombre*.

O: No. He isn't.

    [so far, *tracas* and *obvios* are neither *locas* nor *hombres*]

I: So then, *loca* reaches to what part [looking at Figure 1]? Does it include *solapa* or not?

O: *Loca* would include *traca.*

I: Really?!! (surprised)

O: To *traca,* yes. In a general way, *loca* reaches to *traca.* But *buitre* isn't a *loca.* Then, *loca* is synonymous with "homosexual." *Traca* is also a homosexual. This is the way I see it within Honduran homosexual slang.

[so, now, *tracas* and *obvios* are *locas* or homosexuals]

I: And what is a *loca cuadrada?*

O: A *loca cuadrada* would be like a *solapa.* He's very masculine.

I: *De closet.*

O: Yes. He's *de closet.* He's masculine...

I: Here [Table 1] there should be a thick line between *buitre* and *traca* that would divide *hombres* to one side and *locas* to the other. *Tracas* are bisexuals as *hombres, buitres,* but there is a radical difference based on—

O:—Based on the fact of being penetrated.

I: And that's the difference between the *hombre* and the *loca,* right?

O: Right. That's the difference.

I: This is, that's the most important difference.

O: Yes, although there are some exceptions to the rule, because sometimes *buitres* want to be penetrated, but that's a different story...

...

I: And if an *hombre* wants to be penetrated, is he not an *hombre* anymore?

O: No, say, because it's very difficult to rigidly define people like that because individual human beings tend to change. Only in the [realm of] intimacy does each person knows where to be placed. Only the partner of that person knows his place, indeed.

I: By the way, now I recall when...Dmitri, that boy, the first time...you called him *buitre.* Later...you thought he was *solapa.* And a third time...you said he was *traca.*

O: No. Say, when I learned a[bout him], someone told me that he [Dmitri] was the *buitre* of so-and-so...Then when I saw him walking after you, I thought he was *traca*.

I: *Solapa?*

O: No.

I: I remember the first time you saw him you said he was *solapa.*

O: Yes, *solapa,* but with a tendency to be a *traca.*

I: This is...you went from an extreme to the other [from *buitre* to *solapa*] and later compromised on something intermediate [*traca*].

O: Yeah, exactly. Yes, because [he] was like indefinite. The "gaydar" [*mariconómetro*] didn't give me an exact co-ordinate. I was disoriented.

I: Do you still think he's a *traca?*

O: Yes. I think so. I would bet with 100 per cent certainty that he's *traca.*

The lengthy interview excerpts from Osvaldo show that the major dividing line between a *loca* and an *hombre* is determined by whether someone is considered a penetrator or a penetrated at the level of **public** presentation and conception, regardless of what he does sexually in private. There are *hombres* who have been penetrated in the privacy of a bedroom who are still considered penetrators at the public level. "In longer-term relationships, the *activo* may relax: not always require payment, become more passionately involved, and—if the approach is gradual and does not challenge his masculine self-image—allow penetration. Keeping up appearances (for masculine reputations) is more important than what actually happens in the dark or behind closed doors," as Murray (2000:270) wrote.

In the *ambiente* there is no established category for someone who identifies as homosexual but who likes to play the role of the penetrator. I did meet a couple of young men in the *ambiente* who used the term *gay activo,* to define themselves as homosexuals who penetrate. The concept is entering the *ambiente,* as it has done it in other parts of Latin America (see Murray and Arboleda 1995) and in a few years it might become more commonly used. The Honduran men who told me they were *gay activos* also have sex with women, so they are also behaviorally bisexuals and as such may fall in the category of *"hombres."*

Table One summarizes the *loca* schema of the roles, which are not fixed over time (a person's "sexual career") and not hermetic, mutually exclusive categories. Rows 1-4 are native categorizations. Rows 5-8 are my own interpretations of these categorizations. Only the first column (left to right), *cuadrado*, applies to *hombres* out of the homosexual *ambiente*. All the other columns are within the *ambiente*. Categories for or "real" men fill the first four columns (left to right). *Buitres* and *maridos* are part of *parchís*, so they share similar characteristics. The rightmost three columns are devoted to different types of *locas*. *Traca* (column 5) is ambiguous and occupies an intermediate, often switching position between the categories of *hombre* and *loca*. The rightmost two columns correspond to categories that have been traditionally marginalized from society at large.

Table 1

1. *Cuadrado*	*Parchís*	*Buitre* (zopilote)	*Marido*	*Traca* (plapla)	*Solapa* (de closet)	*Obvio*	*Travesti*
2. no *ambiente*	*ambiente*	*ambiente*	*ambiente*	*ambiente*	*ambiente*	*ambiente*	*ambiente*
3. *hombre*	hombre	hombre	hombre	hombre?! loca?	loca	loca	loca
4. *hombre-hombre*	hombre-hombre	hombre-hombre	hombre-hombre	hombre-hombre?	hombre	hombre	hombre
5. male, man	male, man	male, man	male, man	male, man?	male, non-man	male, non-man	male, non-man
6. penetrator	penetrator	penetrator	penetrator	versatile	penetrated	penetrated	penetrated
7. non-marginalized	non-marginalized	non-marginalized	non-marginalized	non-marginalized	non-marginalized	marginalized	marginalized
8. heterosexual, any age	bisexual, young (15-25 y.o.)	bisexual, young (15-25 y.o.)	bisexual, young (15-25 y.o.)	bisexual, older (30-up)	homosexual any age, usually younger than traca	homosexual any age	homosexual any age

Although the final specification was elicited from Osvaldo, all the terms were used by other *locas* with substantially similar meanings, though others (and, for that matter, Osvaldo on different days) might differ about the boundaries between categories. Despite the representation with lines between categories, these should not be understood as completely solid boundaries. As Murray (1998a:231n40) wrote, "Adjudicating border disputes among arcane combinations of features is rarely how categories are used in naturally-occurring interaction," and

> Fitting nature into perfectly discrete categories does not appear to be how cognition operates—even for phenomena for which there are clear extra-linguistic standards to contrast with lexicons, such as color.... Folk theories implicit in everyday categorisation are not completely articulated logical sets of rules capable of generating clear answers to any question about any imaginable combination of 'essential' social features any more than of 'essential' features of life-forms. Anthropologists' concerns to the contrary notwithstanding, social categories are not designed to adjudicate boundary disputes to such conflicting answers as one is likely to elicit with such questions as, "Is your mother's stepbrother's wife's adopted son from a previous marriage a 'first cousin'?" (1983:398)

Social categories have fuzzy, permeable boundaries but may have agreed-upon "good examples," prototypes about which there is consensus among those using a set of categories (*locas*, in the present instance). A substantial anthropological literature shows higher consensus among experts (here, locas who spend much time in the homosexual *ambiente*), has exhumed the primary informant as a source of cultural data.[8]

---

8.   Berlin (1992); Boster (1985, 1986); Romney, Weller and Batchelder (1986)are foundational works on which much more was built; a particularly elaborate instance is Bernard and Salinas Pedraza 1989.

Agency and authenticity in *locas*

There is no such thing as complete sexual/gender authenticity in a culture of double standards where sexual ideal norms are unrealistic at best. This is particularly true for people who live alternative sexualities. In 1994 I interviewed Carioco, an active member of the "Honduran Association of Homosexuals Against AIDS" (Fernández-Alemany 1995). I started the interview by asking, "Some people call you Paulina. Do you like it being called Paulina?" He replied,

> Well, I don't like it, but it doesn't bother me either. This is just part of a situation we are living in our country, in which the homosexual [male] has to adopt a feminine attitude. Because if he doesn't, he is not accepted in society. If the homosexual is a bit masculine, he is oftentimes rejected, even by the other homosexuals, because traditionally, patriarchal and machistic Honduran society has taught homosexual [males] that they should behave as women. And this has been done so, more than anything else, to submit homosexual males to the rules of society, because women [and, by extension, womanly men] are considered inferior to men. Should the homosexual [male] consider himself an *hombre*, this would be like putting himself at the same level of heterosexual males, and this is something Honduran society doesn't want to see. This is why people allow and encourage the femininity of the homosexual; to keep him controlled, so he wouldn't fight for his rights.

Prieur argued that *locas* or *jotas* do not have a consistent self:

> The self is created in an interplay between the image one gives of oneself and the image one perceives that others have of oneself. If the two do not correspond, the others' response to the image cannot sustain the self. As the family members are *significant others*, in the [George Herbert] Meadian sense, it is important that they know about the son's homosexuality, since a life in complete inauthenticity would be a very painful alternative. But the *jotas* tone down their femininity at home, out of respect for their parents. By

contrast, among strangers they tone down their masculinity, concealing it underneath wigs, foam-rubber padding, and makeup.
The strangers may then respond positively to their femininity, but
this only partly corresponds to their own self-perception. In such a
situation, a consistent self would be difficult to maintain—were it
not for the friends, these people who know "who they really are,"
who respond to all aspects of them. (1998:102)

San Pedro *locas* generally claim that they consciously manipulate
their femininity **and** their masculinity, depending on the context.
Therefore it is not a matter of toning down or concealing what they
"really are," but a matter of acting according to what is more conventional for the situation—a matter of conscious choice. Nonetheless,
one may wonder if there is something of truth in the statement of
manipulating or molding an already established nature. If not, why are
they *locas* in the first place and not *hombres*? But the origins of the
actual differentiation of *locas* and *hombres* are too obscure to be determined here (see Prieur 1998:104-139 for a valiant attempt to do so)
and they do not necessarily have to do with innate features, but could
be related as well to interactional, sociocultural factors—or a combination of all of the above.

Two excerpts from an interview with Horacio illustrate the agency
of the *loca* when it comes to his public presentation of femininity:

INTERVIEWER: You said that you tried to behave as masculine
as possible in certain situations. How is that?
HORACIO: In certain situations. This is, according to me, right?
But, I look quite feminine and everyone knows it. But people love
the seriousness with which I present myself. This lets them see the
difference between a man and a woman. Because of my
nature—male—they think they are talking to a man, right?
Although visually they get confused sometimes. Do you understand?
I: Are you saying the opposite of what you told me before? You are
saying now that you have a feminine appearance but the way you

carry yourself is masculine?

H: I have to do it because of the society in which I live.

I: Before you said that your nature was masculine but your thinking was feminine.

H: Feminine, exactly, but with my partners. [With them] I act like a woman…but [in] my social life I try to project myself as a male, this is, leaving on one side every trace of femininity; I mean, mannerisms, expressions, ahm, gestures, all those things.

I: Also everything that may make a reference to homosexuality?

H: That too. Everything that may make a reference to homosexuality.

I: Does this include the life with your family?

H: Yeah.

I: So you establish a difference between your life with your partner and your public life…

H: My public life, exactly. Not completely public, though. When it's time to perform as an entrepreneur, as a businessman, yes. I have to project myself with strength. Because business people like to deal with strong people. Because if you go with weaknesses, like for example, if you are too feminine…you are not going to do anything. But if you have, let's say, if you have a feminine projection, but you behave with strength, like you are man-to-man, they respect you more. They take you more into consideration and they make good business with you. But if not they say, "I can take advantage of this one." Do you understand?

…

I: I'm interested in the distinction between public and private. You say that in the public world one finds the business world, your work, where you present yourself as masculine to be taken seriously, you said. But your family—is it also part of this world? How so?

H: Ahm, yes, that's a part of my family life, because there [in my family] I also act the same, this is, I try to be strong, to not show my weaknesses. To make them see that they are with a brother, not with a sister, do you understand? It is very contradictory all what I'm saying, but it's the truth.

I: Then, besides the dating arena, are there other areas where you would show your femininity or homosexuality?

H: No, no, no. About my femininity, only 100 per cent when I am with my partner.

I: What about with your friends, with your homosexual friends?

H: No. With my homosexual friends I believe I am "normal." I think I am always "normal" and only like that [effeminate] with my partner or with men I deal with to whom I have to show that image.

I: You **have** to show that image?

H: Ahm, yes, because I think that if I am with a sex that I like, I have to show what I really feel, how I feel, because I have to make them feel attracted to me at any rate, right? So I have to use my femininity, because if I **use** my masculinity I will go nowhere.

What he feels that motivates feminine self-presentation is homosexual attraction. Horacio uses femininity to seduce men. At least for him, homosexual desire is primary and feminine self-presentation a means rather than an end in-itself. He does not have any sense of being a female in a male body.

Compulsory passivity and the power of penetration

Paraphrasing Leo Bersani, Lee Edelman (1994:98) claimed that for a man, "getting fucked" is seen as a suicidal act because it implies that he is being inscribed in the role of the woman—a passive object—that, by extension, "connotes a willing sacrifice of the subjectivity, the disciplined self-mastery, traditionally attributed only to those who perform the 'active' or penetrative—and hence 'masculine'—role in the active-passive binarism that organizes 'our' cultural perspective on sexual behavior."

Condemning the "'addictive' passivity of the anus in intercourse" and linking it to AIDS, is a form of strengthening the male heterosexual's moral agency which feels constantly threatened in "our" society, Edelman claimed (101). "Only *against* women and gay men may the 'normal male subject' imagine himself to be a subject at all" (105). Edelman, attributed gay men's penetrability to their loss of subjectivity and agency in the eyes of society, especially from the viewpoint of heterosexual male insertors.

It is hard to determine to what extent exclusive passivity is a choice or a cultural imperative in the case of Honduran *locas*. *Locas* seem to enjoy being penetrated and I have seen many intentionally manipulate gender markers that will mark them as penetrable in Honduran contexts. So I doubt that passivity is as compulsory as Edelman claims it to be.

On the other hand, I can see how passivity is culturally condemned and an oxymoron for an *hombre* or man, so that in some sense *hombres* need *locas* to define themselves: as being not-*locas*. That is, by not being sexually penetrable, *hombres* become *hombres*.

There is an explanation for a functional role of male sexual passivity in Latin American: sexual passivity in some males accommodates the need for sexual release of young, heterosexually-identified males who do not have access to women because of their age, social conditions, religion, or lack of money. In his study of sexual behavior among males of middle and lower-class in the northwestern regions of Mexico, Carrier (1995) found that the incidence of same-sex sex in males was extremely high among young, unmarried males. These males cannot have sexual relations with their girlfriends or most other women because "good" women are supposed to remain virgins until they get married. On the other hand, they cannot afford "bad" women (prostitutes) either, because they are too expensive. These men learned from an early age that "homosexual," sexually passive males, are available as sexual outlets. In this region, same-sex sex is acceptable as long as it is not acknowledged publicly (16, 188). Even though the homosexual relationships that Carrier observed in Mexico in most cases occurred between consenting partners, one should not overlook the fact that (a) many of the homosexuals who play the passive role have been sexually abused by *hombres*, especially during childhood; (b) many of the *hombres* see and treat the passive homosexual with contempt as an compelling testament to their power and superiority; and (c) at least for certain cases, the effeminate (or homosexually-identified) man is compulsorily made passive by other people and society at large. I remember talking to two Latino gay men who prefer to be tops. When they initiated their homosexual careers in their respective countries (Mexico and Honduras) they played only the passive role, because they thought that it was the only available way to be homosexual. Only after moving to the US did they realize that they did not need to be exclusively passive to be homosexuals. After that discovery, they realized that what they actually enjoyed the most was the active or penetrator's role. Had they stayed in their countries of origin, they would have perhaps always remained trapped within the regime of compulsory passivity. Or perhaps they would have become acculturated enough to the *ambiente* to find out that there actually was a broad spectrum of possibilities awaiting for them in the continuum *hombre/loca*.

Just as there may be *locas* who feel "naturally" inclined to be effeminate and are compulsorily made sexually passive by societal enculturation, there may be others who feel "naturally" inclined to be sexually passive and adopt feminine gender markers to attract penetrators. Moreover, there may be a majority of homosexuals who feel a combination of these and other desires.

According to psychoanalyst Bossio Montellanos (1992:75), "the explanation for effeminate behavior in men who seek to attract other men, lies precisely on the desire to capture male attention by highlighting what for men results erotic…. Thus, transvestism does not reveal so much the individual as it does his context…Both "femininity" and "masculinity" are cultural imperatives, which validity has to do with the subjects' need of social integration. The existence of women and men who transgress these roles in order to approach people of their same sex confirms the efficacy of such roles' fixation process as cultural values."

6

"DEL OTRO LADO": THE VIEW OF HONDURAN MALES WHO PENETRATE "HOMOSEXUALS"

O utside the *ambiente*, in the general population, the criterial feature of being fully an *hombre* is siring sons. According to Gilmore (1990:41), paternity is the key test in the circum-Mediterranean machismo complex: "In those parts of southern Europe where the Don Juan model of sexual assertiveness is highly valued, a man's assigned task is not just to make endless conquests but to spread his seed. Beyond mere promiscuity, the ultimate test is that of competence in reproduction.... The Mediterranean emphasis on manliness means results: it means procreating offspring (preferably boys). At the level of community endorsement, it is legitimate reproductive success, more than simply erotic acrobatics—a critical fact often overlooked by experts on Mediterranean honor." Requirements for this evidence increase with ages, and the *hombres* in the *ambiente* are of an age less than that at which it becomes criterial. (Also see Bourdieu 2000:12.) Based on fieldwork in Mexico City, Guttman (1996) also downplayed sexual conquests as central to "the meaning of *macho*." He stressed that being able to provide for and protect the children one has sired is also very important. Murray (2000:275) characterized this as "the expectation of social as well as biological paternity [is] part of the male role for Latinos."

For *locas, hombre* is the class of suitably masculine (impenetrable) husbands. But what do the partners of the Honduran homosexuals think about manhood and the possibility of their own self-identifications as *hombres* being compromised by sexual and romantic relationships with unpenetrative males? This chapter delves into the self-representations and sexual ideologies of *hombres* who share their penises (and, in some cases, hearts) with homosexual males. It is primarily based on the seven formal interviews eliciting sexual life histories and conceptions of homosexuality. Although the fundamental penetrator/penetrated dichotomy is basic for these *hombres*, they show no interest or negative interest in males who in Prieur's view "steal femininity" (i.e., "obvious" or transvestite males).

In contrast to Carrier's (1995:198, 205) difficulty in getting *mayates* (Mexican macho insertors) to be interviewed and to Kulick, who gave up on trying to get the partners of Brazilian *travestis* to talk about their sexual histories and ideas, and even to the embarrassed skittishness Prieur (1998:179-223) found among the male sexual partners kept by Mexican *travestis*, I found these Honduran men willing to discuss their sexual histories and beliefs/attitudes.

Sometimes the abstractness of some of my queries puzzled these *hombres*, but they were very willing to tell me who did what to whom and in what position(s). I am not certain that their sexual relationships unfolded in precisely the ways that they recalled to me, but for trying to understand the schematization of the rights and obligations of sexual roles within Honduran sexual culture(s), the factual reliability about behavior is less important for a study of sexual culture than what they believe about their conduct and ongoing relationships to their male and female sexual partners.

What draws lone wolves to hunt and feed on homosexual males?

Hombres' socialization into the *hombre* role in homosexual relations(/ships) is primarily by their homosexual partners. *Hombres* who are in homosexual relationships do not hang out together. Whereas, across Latin America, *pasivos* socialize and clump together in cruising grounds, *activos* hunt singly, don't make friends with each other, and don't socialize with each other. The Costa Rican male sex workers studied by Schifter consider socializing with their homosexual clients "outside the brothel means homosexualizing themselves" and being gossiped about by the homosexuals (Schifter and Aggleton 1999:144). Arboleda wrote of the same pattern in Lima, Peru:

> *Activos* play their role carefully, so as not to implicate themselves too much with the *ambiente*. They do not cruise with friends and would feel awkward being observed by their friends or convincing them to go cruising together. In any case, prowling alone marks someone in the *ambiente* as an *activo*. As Joselito put it, "What else could he be doing alone?" (1995:104)

One result of the lack of socializing among those who act as *hombres* with homosexual males is that the *hombres* have less elaborated typologies of sexualities than the *homosexuales* do. The *hombres* sometimes also have idiosyncratic understandings of labels—and of the boundaries and requirements of their role within homosexual relationships.

Six of the seven *hombres* reported having sexual intercourse with females before having any kind of sex with males. The range in age for first vaginal penetration was 7-16 years of age (median 11, mean 10.3). The first sexual encounters with males that the other six recalled was four or more years later: at ages ranging between 14 and 20 (median 17, mean 16.3). All but one of the first female partners and all but one of the first male partners was three or more years older than the boy(ish) penetrator.[1]

While most of the *hombres* I interviewed told me about the tight anus being more pleasurable to penetrate than the loose vagina is (an account the *homosexuales* eagerly advance), *hombres* generally seemed to place more importance on friendship than on anything else in their positive evaluation of homosexual partners. Allan told me that the reason he prefers to date a homosexual is that the friendship of a homosexual is much more reliable than is that of a woman.

Jaime explained that homosexuals are more honest than women are, and that it is easier to communicate with them than it is to communicate with women, especially about sexual desires and fantasies.

> INTERVIEWER: Of the sex you have had with women and with men, which gave you more pleasure?
> JAIME: The person is special. Because I passed four years with my partner, he gave me more pleasure. Why? Because we lived together a long time and I experienced knowing him as a person and that enhanced the pleasure.... You can discuss things with (male) partner, but not with women: fundamental things, you know like satisfying [one] better because women never discuss it [giving or receiving sexual pleasure].

Cáceres and Jiménez 1999:186) quote a Peruvian male sex worker's very similar view: "More confidence exists with a guy in the sense that you can speak about anything, you can do everything."

As in other interviews with *hombres*, Jaime contrasted women in general to his specific homosexual partner. The "sample" of women with whom he (or the other *hombres*) had been intimate was small, but the basis for generalizing about "homosexuals" was even smaller.

In an extended variation on Voltaire's "once a philosopher [studying variety in the world], twice a pervert," *hombres* are (in the homosexual

---

1.   This patterning parallels the self-reports by the penetrators of transvestites Prieur interviewed: "The seven mayates I interviewed are between 17 and 23 years old. Six of them told that the first time they had sex, it was with a woman; 5 of the 6 had been between 11 and 16 years old. The first same-sex experience had for most of them taken place at about 16" (1998:214).

view) supposed to like many women, but to make an exception for a maximum of only one specific, very special homosexual. Gastón, a homosexually identified man who had been in a one-year relationship with a "heterosexual" man when I interviewed him, told me about his *hombre*: "He doesn't like men. He doesn't like them. It is only me [he likes]"). Helmer made the same claim for his *hombre*: his partner feels sexually attracted to all or most women, he has fallen in love and been in a relationship only with Helmer. When I asked Jaime, "Have you had relations with other men?", he replied: "No. I have not had any. This is the only experience in my life of that." Somewhat reluctantly, he speculated about the possibility of a relationship with another male partner that was even more explicit about the qualities of the specific individual that matter: "I believe that it is the person, not the class of person (that matters), because if he is not a person whose ways I find agreeable, I could never start" a relationship.

Similarly, when I asked Enrique: "Sometimes, is there a man you find attractive?", he replied: "No. I have seen men who could have good physiques, but they do not attract me, or draw my attention." Alexander and Gerson also stated that they were not attracted to other homosexuals than their respective partners.

Some *hombres* argue that, because of AIDS, they would only feel safe having sex with their particular homosexual partner and with no one else:

> JAIME: Yes, I have had [sex with a male], but he was my partner, who is the person I've known the best; otherwise I wouldn't do it because I'm afraid [to have sex] with someone I don't know.
> INTERVIEWER: Why are you afraid?
> J: One could get too many diseases. These days HIV/AIDS and other STDs are far too common here in Honduras, especially in San Pedro. Perhaps every day six people die of HIV/AIDS [here]. This is why, when I feel desire or something like that, or perhaps I want to experience that, I look for the person I already know.
> I: So sometimes it happens to you that you feel desire to have sex

with another man?

J: Yes, I mean, [I feel desire] to penetrate the person I have already been with.

I: So it isn't just any man, but him.

J: Yes, it isn't just any man; only him. I have fear of other persons I don't know.... Because many diseases can grab onto one.... I only go with the person I know.

The known partner is believed to be safer.[2] After extolling the better treatment and understanding homosexuals (in contrast to women) give men, Allan volunteered that homosexuals in general are safer (for avoiding HIV-transmission) than women in general:

ALLAN: I believe that one risks more dangers with a woman than with a homosexual.

I: In what sense?

A: In diseases, in venereal diseases. I believe. I don't know for sure.

I: Why?

A: In that most women are not careful, they don't take precautions like homosexuals do. Homosexuals, now, frequently get tested for AIDS. [inaudible] There is more danger of disease with a woman than with a homosexual.

I: But you can have sex with protection with a woman or with a man.

A: No. Always with both kinds **always** [I use] protection.

Being treated especially well by their homosexual partners was even more of a leitmotif than the claim that homosexual partners constitute a lower danger of disease than female sexual partners do. As Allan put it: "Another man appreciates a man more, right? Also they make one feel better than a woman does, understand? .... The friendship of homosexuals is excellent. They are nicer to you than a woman is."

2.   The success of the early "promiscuity paradigm" (see Murray 1996a:88-108) continues to provide a false sense of security rationalizing unprotected sex with someone guessed/hoped to be HIV-.

Enrique also stressed the specialness of his *homosexual* partner:

INTERVIEWER: Was it only sex, or was it more than that?
ENRIQUE: I think it was, uhm, a relationship.
I: Why?
E: I think that the relationship exists, because I like the affection
(*cariño*) from him, I like how he treats me, I liked his personality,
this is why I always—I mean, he, he is the only one who, the only
homosexual with whom I've made the sex and mmm (clearing his
throat), the only one that I've met who's been sincere.
I: Have you met other homosexuals after him?
E: Yes, I've met other homosexuals but, uhm, no, I haven't dared
to have [sexual] relations with other homosexuals. I have only
talked to them, they have told me that they like how I look and
that they want to have sex with me, but I told them no. That for
me there has only been one homosexual, and there isn't gonna be
second, though they ask it of me. This is what I tell them....
If I see homosexuals in the street who are attractive and all that, I
might like to be crude with them and say stupid things, but to
have relations? No. Because, once one has staked out a position
[established a relationship] with someone and one does not know
what else, so it is dangerous.

Jaime also spoke about his homosexual partner as being "a sincere
friend," and told me how his partner is able to communicate with him
and how older gays friends (in their 30s and 40s) give him useful
advice, unlike friends of his own age. Jaime also asserts the singularity
of the experience of his special relationship (of four year's duration):

I: The only partner you have had is a man?
J: Yes. This is the only partner I've had.
I: And have you had sexual relations with other men?
J: No. I have not had any. This is the only experience in my life of
a relationship with a man.

Freddie similarly stressed that the friendship of homosexuals/women/travestis (he does not distinguish kinds of non-*hombres*) is good, and mentioned in particular that Helvecio gives him good advice. And although he said he felt admiration "for some who look beautiful (*bonitos* [masculine])," he repeatedly stressed that for him knowing well and feeling comfortable with the person is more important than any physical characteristics (including natal/biological sex).

José told me that friendship with a homosexual was better than friendship with other *hombres* (rivals) or with women (who tend to be jealous of his relationships with other women. His view is that "a homosexual will not envy my being a man or having a desire for women." He also said that majority of his friends are gay males.

Comparing the pleasures of penetrating women and homosexuals

Although, in the abstract, sex with females is supposed to be better, for the *hombres* who penetrate (and are never penetrated by) homosexuals whom I interviewed, there were aspects of sex that are better with women and others that are better with homosexual males. Overall, the biological sex of their sexual partners was less important than friendship relationships with particular persons. (Although sometimes referring to their male partners as *hombres*, these men often used "person" (*persona*)—which is feminine in grammatical gender in Spanish—to refer to their homosexual partner.)

Despite mentioning that anuses are tighter than vaginas, José said that penetrating a male was not necessarily more pleasurable than penetrating a female and penetrating a female was not necessarily more pleasurable than penetrating a male.

Allan recalled that, at least the first time he anally penetrated a homosexual, "I was aroused and tried to make it, to have relations with him. It was the first time. I penetrated in his ass, something I had not done before. It hurt a little, for the first time, right?"

One young *hombre*, who said sex with his homosexual male partner was better, reversed the usual contrast of tight sphincter and loose vagina:

> JAIME: The gay gave me more pleasure than the woman did. Women put up more resistance to making love with me. There are, perhaps, women who do not resist my penis when it was erect. There are some who say "I'm married." And the man, no.
> I: You have a big penis?
> J: It is not extremely large, but perhaps the women are tight.
> I: Isn't your partner tight?
> J: But he does it with love.

Even this is less about bodily pleasure and pain than the greater complaisance of a specific male partner in contrast to female resistance that is represented as being more attitudinal than physical—in line with how respectable women are supposed to be: chaste before marriage and frigid after it, never seeking physical pleasure in sex (Stevens 1973:96).

Later in the same interview, Jaime provided the more conventional contrast:

> I: Are there any differences between what you feel during anal sex and vaginal sex?
> J: The opening is tighter in the man than in the woman. For this, sex with a male is better. It feels tight, a woman, no. The woman feels loose and also wet.
> I: And you don't like that?
> J: No, I don't like that.
> I: So what will you do when you are married? [He had said that he expected to get married after completing military service.]
> J: I'll get used to it.

Alexander did not raise the criterion of tightness of fit. I asked him: "What gives you more pleasure?" After a long pause, he said, "Most if it is oral," which I mistook to be a preference rather than a statement about frequency. I continued by asking whether there are differences in pleasure from oral sex depending upon the sex of the fellator. First he made clear who was doing whom, and then we got to his preference for sex of fellator:

> I: Do you have oral sex with women?
> A: No. I don't have oral sex with them, but they do with me. Some have asked for it, but I don't do that.
> I: Do you like it—being fellated by women?
> A: Yes.
> I: Is oral sex different from a woman than from a homosexual?
> A: It is different: it is better from a homosexual.[3]

He also preferred homosexual males to women for anal sex:

> I: Have you had anal sex with women?
> A: Some [two].
> I: Is anal sex different from a woman than from a homosexual?
> A: It feels more different because, we say the homosexual moves while the woman does not. So it's not as exciting. I like it better with a homosexual than with a woman. [Later, he noted that women move when being penetrated vaginally, but in his experience not when being anally penetrated.]
> I: Of all the types of sex—vaginal, anal with a woman, anal with men, oral with a man, oral with a woman—what gives you the greatest pleasure?
> A: Anal sex with a homosexual. Anal more than oral.

And at another juncture in the interview:

---

3.   This is also the conventional wisdom among the Costa Rican male sex workers in Casa Lila: "'Women do not know how to suck,' said Miguel. Rodrigo agreed that women do not 'have experience'" and, thus, lack expertise in oral ministrations (Schifter and Aggleton 1999:147). Lila, the male bordello owner, said that "what 'hooks' some otherwise heterosexual men on male sex work is the quality of oral sex that clients provide: 'Women do not know hot to suck and the youngsters go crazy with the clients' expertise'" (146). Also see Prieur (1998:211).

> I: Do you feel more attracted to a woman or a man, or a woman or
> a homosexual.
> A: For the aspects that I like best, homosexuals.

Later in the interview, he reiterated this preference ("For the aspects
[of sexual relations] that I like best, homosexuals") and gave as the reason: "It's more romantic." That is, for Alexander also, the physical differences between male and female bodies (and, specifically, orifices) are
less important than feelings.

Enrique stressed affection and being appreciated, to the verge of
being venerated by his homosexual partner:

> I: Could you compare the relations you have had with the homo-
> sexual with those with women? What are the differences and simi-
> larities?
> ENRIQUE: The difference between a homosexual and a woman
> is, for me, it is the affection (*cariño*). The love that he has, because
> a woman treats you differently than a homosexual (does).
> I: How?
> E: Because, mmm, a homosexual gives you your space as a man,
> and cherishes you, and speaks beautifully [flatteringly], and, again,
> gives you the space as a man who is special.... The woman does
> not.

He said that there are not differences in pleasure between penetrating male and female bodies:

> Sex with both [the woman who provided anal and oral sex and the
> homosexual] are equally good, equally exciting. My moment of
> weakness is when my penis is being sucked.
> I had more pleasure with the homosexual than with the first two
> women [who only permitted vaginal penetration]. The only differ-
> ence is that a woman's body is smoother [than a homosexual
> man's]. My pleasure is not affected by whether the body [being
> penetrated] is that of a man or of a woman.

Later he mentioned that his penis slid more easily into a woman and that penetrating an anus hurts his penis at first:

I: Painful to you?
E: Yes, when introducing it, it hurts [me] some.... [Once inside] for me the pleasure is the same, equal pleasure....

After he said that he liked to penetrate face-to-face, I asked:

I: In that position you can see his genitals, no?
E: Yes, but they are covered with a towel, so there is no problem. At times I look casually at them and may touch them when moving, but no, it doesn't bother me, it's not a problem....
[If the homosexual turns over and his male genitals are visible it is] a little odd but, later, no, later it doesn't seem important that you have made it with another male (*hombre*).

He does not kiss his homosexual male partner (he kisses women). He said, "an *hombre* kissing an *hombre* would be ugly," and, at another point that before having sex with him, he told the male who became his partner that he thought that an *hombre* with and *hombre* would look very ugly. (In both instances, he did not distinguish homosexual from *hombre*). When he tried sex with the homosexual, however, "it felt good. It did not feel weird (*raro*)."

José, who also enjoys penetrating males from the front, raising their legs, similarly denied any interest in homosexuals' genitals:

I: Do you look at their genitals?
JOSÉ: No, because they cover them with a towel.
I: And if they don't (cover them), do you like at them?
J: No, never. I would be traumatized and wouldn't be able to do anything.
I: Do you ever touch their genitals.
J: No, never.

Allan opined that kissing is better with a woman, noting without elaborating that "not all homosexuals can be kissed on the mouth, only some." However, he said that sex with homosexual males is safer than sex with women and that the friendship of homosexual males is better than that of women.

The *hombre* whom I interviewed who was most explicit about liking to touch and kiss his homosexual partner was also the one who enumerated the most ways in which female bodies (in general) are more pleasing than male homosexual ones. Like Allan, Gerson mentioned that kissing is better with a woman. Almost immediately, however, he all but retracted this view: "With my homosexual partner, I have kissed mouth to mouth, it doesn't feel the same, because he has a mustache and I have a mustache. So I don't like it. But nevertheless always a mouth is a mouth and a tongue is a tongue, no? So it feels the same, no? The only difference, perhaps, is the mustache." He also noted that having sex with his homosexual partner "feels different because my partner is hairy. The body of women is not hairy."[4] He also added that women "have tits to touch, right?" though he also likes to kiss the chest and touch the buttocks of his homosexual partner.

He also indicated that a woman proficient at fellatio and willing to perform it would be better (than his current sexual options), though sexual relations with his homosexual partner are "excellent":

I: Why don't you just have sex with men or only with women. What is different?

---

4. Later in the interview, in the context of appreciating his homosexual partner's masculinity, I returned to the subject of his partner's hairy body:
   G: No one would think that.
   M: And you like that about him.
   G: That is what I like most about him, that he does not
   look like a *travesti*.
   M: You like his hairy body?
   G: The body of him?
   M: You said that he is hairy.
   G: Yes.
   M: It pleases you
   G: Yes, it pleases me (*me gusta*).

G: There is an aspect of the woman, if she is going to do every-thing—if she is willing to provide oral sex—while a homosexual can not do all.

I: Why?

G: Because I cannot kiss the parts he has.... But the rest, all is excellent.

I: What is the rest?

G: It's good, the relations we have: sexual, friendly, understanding.

I: But my question is: are there some pleasures that are different in homosexual relations that you do not obtain in heterosexual rela-tions.

G: Truly, I have no answer to that, because the relation that I have with a homosexual, it pleases me to have and if I could only be with him, I could have it only with him. But also, women please me and I have my partner who is homosexual and I have the rela-tionship with my woman, no? I have good relations with both. There's no problem. We get along well.

I: Is there some pleasure that feels different, richer?

G: They are totally different. Because the woman makes love in one way, while the homosexual makes it in another. Both give me pleasure and I like both forms.

I: The pleasures are not equal, not the same—

G: Not the same, because with women one is aroused more, while with a homosexual one is aroused, feeling pleasure, but not like with a woman....

The pleasure is always great from having the anus. Anal sex feels the same, no? With a homosexual. Because it is the same, it is always the anus, right? But what feels different with a woman is that the woman has a more aroused sound, do you understand?

Crying out—even screaming—enhances Gerson's pleasure. In addi-tion to doing this more often or more volubly, the other advantage women have is the fullness of their breasts. Gerson explained, "my homosexuals does not have well-developed breasts like a woman."

Nonetheless, he said that he likes to touch his homosexual partner's body. And he likes the certainty one has with a homosexual but not with a woman that sexual access will be provided to him:

I: What do you feel when you have sex with a homosexual?

G: What does it make me feel? If we have enough time for that, it makes me feel neither good nor bad, no? I feel relaxed, no?

I: And at the start?

G: At the start—At the start, if I have the certainty that I will go to bed with a man—it pleases me and it doesn't embarrass me.

I: Why? What it is that makes you happy, gives you pleasure, and for what reason?

G: In the first place, happy, and that, perhaps, one has the chance to have sex, to have a good time, and pleasure, because both take pleasure in it.... I feel good, because if one is going to have a relationship with a homosexual, one knows what is going to happen, right? and one does not feel penitent about doing that: I have never felt guilty about what I've done.

Contrary to the norms for *hombre* detachment from any homosexual partner, Gerson was willing to say he liked to touch his homosexual partner's buttocks and chest: "My homosexuals does not have well-developed breasts like a woman.... but I still like to touch his body" and also kissed mouth to mouth. Although he likes the "more aroused sound" and larger breasts of women, Gerson stated that he was in love with his homosexual partner, and not with his female partner:

I: Are you in love (*enamorado*) with your homosexual partner.

G: Yes. Because I am only with him. I have relations with him.

I: What does "enamorado" mean to you?

G: Love—both giving love and understanding. And, most of all, not only to be a partner but also friends.

I: Are you in love with your female partner?

G: I like her, but I am not in love with her, if you understand me, but I like (*quiero,* which can also mean want/desire) her.

I:…Do you feel love for her?

G: Yes, but it is sexual, nothing more. I'm beginning to be, but it [the relationship] is new, less than two months.

And, while expecting to marry and sire children, Gerson believes he could be happy without heterosexual relations or without homosexual relations:

I: Can you imagine living your life solely with your homosexual partner or solely with the woman?

G: I've never thought about it, but in that case I could have a happy life with my homosexual partner. [Note which hypothetical he answers first.]

I: Do you believe you could have one with your male partner?

G: Yes.

I: And do you believe you could have only a female partner and not have a homosexual partner?

G: If I wanted to, yes, I could have one.

I: And you would feel happy?

G: Yes. Why not?…. I could live my life with only my (homosexual) partner or with only my female (partner).

This does not mean that Gerson is contemplating modern gay reciprocity and doing anything with the male genitalia of his homosexual partner:

I: Have you touched the genitals of a homosexual some time?

G: Only grazed, I am not accustomed to touching them, I would not want to.

I: Sucking?

G: Never.

Jaime said that he liked and appreciated, but was not in love with (enamorado) with his homosexual partner of four years, who as a very special—indeed, in Jaime's view unique—person who liked and appreciated Jaime very much and with whom Jaime was able to communicate well. Not only is this homosexual the only one for Jaime, but Jaime believes that he is the only *hombre* for his homosexual. (Gerson also maintained that he was the first *hombre* with whom his homosexual partner had ever had sex.) Jaime could not say whether his homosexual partner was in love with him or loved him. Kissing was "agreeable, because I know that he is sincere with me, so I ought not to be an egoist with him." But for Jaime, as for Gerson, contact with his partner's penis is only incidental:

> INTERVIEWER: Do you touch his genitals.
> JAIME: No, I've never touched them.
> I: In four years, never?
> J: In four years, never. Because he is the gay, not me. I could not take a hold of his penis.
> I: But you have wanted to do so?
> J: No, I have never wanted to do so—
> I: Because when you are *armas al hombro* [what Jaime had specified as his favorite position, with his partner's legs on his shoulders], his genitals are there, on his stomach.
> J: Yes. They stick to his stomach. But I never masturbate him.
> I: But do you take pleasure in the feeling of grazing against his genitals?
> J: I feel that this is a person who is close to me, in whom I have confidences, so I don't have negative feelings....
> I: Why is *armas al hombro* your favorite position?
> J: I am better able to look at him enjoying it and to feel his excitement and he asks for it and likes it a lot.
> I: Does he have an erection?
> J: Yes, sometimes, I like to see that he is aroused and feels good, and relaxed, everything. We go together well.

Later, when he said that he liked to caress "that which I am going to penetrate," I pressed the question of being aroused by touching a male body. His lawyerly response was: "I am not going to say that I am aroused [by touching a male body], because then I would be entering [the range] of a bisexual, because that is way of feeling of the bisexual.

It was difficult not to take "I am not going to say" as an indirect affirmation of the desire which is supposed to flow only in the other direction (the homosexual's desire for the *hombre*'s body). It is more "I am an *hombre*, and an *hombre* does not feel such desire" than what would be the easy denial "No, I don't feel such desire."

Apparently, his partner did not press Jaime for any sexual reciprocity (which would devalue Jaime in conventional masculinity):

> He was very good with me. He understood everything. He knew that I could not reciprocate because I am all man (*hombre completo*). So [he knew from the outset that] one day I was going to leave and take a woman and have children…that the time to be with him would end.

Similarly, Enrique expressed gratitude at not being pressed to do anything against his (*hombre* penetrative) nature by his considerate homosexual partner: "He always gives me confidence and never makes me obligated. It is always for me to decide: I'm neither worried nor obligated."

These self-consciously masculine young men (*hombres completos*) uniformly denied being attracted to or fantasizing about male bodies. They generally did not want to talk about the bodies of their male homosexual partners, aside from passing mentions of the greater hairiness of male bodies. Recalling one former partner, I prompted Allan to express pleasure at some femininity noticeable to Allan in private:

I: And the third men with whom you have relations was homosexual, but not very obviously, notably—
ALLAN: Yes, it was not very obvious—
I: And some time you noticed that he was feminine?
A: Yes.
I: And you liked it?
A: What?

I: To be with a homosexual who is feminine: you were attracted?

A: Yes. [inaudible] I felt tranquil—If you're asking if I had doubts, no, none.

They did, however, not want homosexual partners in ongoing relationships to be feminine. In particular, they did not want them to cross-dress. They want partners who are literally "passable"—males with whom they can appear in public who are not obviously homosexual and, therefore, do not compromise the public appearance of "normal" masculinity of the *hombres*.

Gerson, after the refrain of "special relationship," commented very specifically on wanting his homosexual partner to look "normal": to protect "my reputation as an *hombre*.... I can not walk with an effeminate male."

I: Why do you believe that you were attracted to him and not to other persons?

G: I don't know. Perhaps because he is special, in the sense that I have confidence in him. And for this reason I like him more.

I: Do you consider him masculine, feminine, normal—

G: I consider him normal.

I: Do you think you would like him if he were more feminine? If he was like a transvestite?

G: No, because I sincerely do not like *travestis*.

I: And if your partner was very macho, very masculine, do you believe that you would feel attracted to him.

G: Yes, because it doesn't embarrass me how he looks in downtown [San Pedro] now, right? It doesn't give me uneasiness. But if there is another homosexual who is too conspicuous—shooting off the feathers, we say—that bothers me, because perhaps there people—friends, whoever—who say: "Your brother is hanging around with homosexuals," and perhaps they do not say homosexual, but say *culero*, right? Words that I do not like to say. So it wouldn't bother me at all to go out with him, even if he were more masculine, even if he were like that. It would bother me if he were like a travesti, yes, that would bother me. But he is like (looks like) a macho.

I: So in passing by, no one would think he is homosexual.

G: No one would think that.

I: And you like that about him?

G: That is what I like **most** about him: that he does not look like a *travesti*.

Jaime also shuddered at the thought of having a relationship with an effeminate homosexual: "I see many men dressed like women, travestis, but they are not attractive to me.... Thank God my partner does not have any problems like that [and, instead, Jaime asserts, appears masculine in the street, so that] we go together to eat, to the cinema, to the capital, to various places."

Jaime said that he liked that his partner "has like the *hombre* boldness. It is not that he is going to penetrate me, rather that I am going to penetrate him. But it pleases me that he has this boldness," rather than the timidity which is attributed to homosexuals in the popular imagination in Honduras (and elsewhere).

Gerson denied feeling attraction for other males' bodies. Although he said he was attracted to his homosexual partner and liked touching him, he also said that he does not get aroused thinking about him or about other male bodies:

I: What do you get from having relations with him.

G: I feel attracted to him, right? I like the way of being with him.

I: What is your fantasy. When you masturbate do you sometimes think of him.

G: No, I never think of him when masturbating.

I: But when you think of something that arouses you, you have someone else in your imagination?

G: No. I only have the relationship (with his partner), nothing more.

....

I: And you didn't like any other person this way?

G: No, I had not wanted that. I touched buttocks, but no, I didn't like it. I did not feel attracted to other persons.

....

I: Are you attracted to *travestis*?

G: No, I only like my partner.

That relationship was what mattered to him, not visual stimuli, also came out in my attempt to probe masturbation fantasies. He said that he did not need to masturbate, having regular male and female sexual partners.[5] When I brought up the spectacle of nude images, he recalled that earlier in his life, he was aroused by female images, but as an adult has put aside such childish stimuli:

I: You have seen magazines with photos of nude men.

G: Yes I have seen them, but they do not turn me on, no. To tell the truth, I don't like to look at them. When I have nothing to do, perhaps, from curiosity, but they do not excite me.

I: And magazines with nude women?

G: Never.

I: They have never aroused you?

G: They do not arouse me.

I: Looking does not arouse you much.

G: Before, yes: I would take a magazine of women that made me hot to the bathroom and masturbated. That was before. Now, no. When one is a young man (*chavalo*), there's much sickness of mind....

I do not have to masturbate.... I always have the same satisfaction and satisfy my partner.

I: Has there ever been a time you masturbated fantasizing about

---

5.   Under further interrogation, he said that last time he had masturbated was five months earlier. When I asked him what he thought about when masturbating, he (again) mentioned a woman crying out in ecstasy as he penetrates her: "A woman starting to cry out. To be blunt that's what I like most to imagine."

him or another man.

G: No.... I never think of him when masturbating.

These men were more reluctant to discuss masturbation than they were to discuss penetrative sex (of any sort with the orifices of males or of females). Enrique said that he thinks of women when masturbating, sometimes a woman with another woman; sometimes, when he only pets with his *novia*, he has wet dreams, he told me. He has never dreamed of having sex with a homosexual, and, masturbating, the only bodies he imagines are female ones.

None of these *hombres* mentioned direct financial benefit from their relations and relationships with homosexuals. Unlike the *cacheros* in Lila's House in San José, Costa Rica (a male bordello studied by Schifter 1998), none asserted that he was only interested in sex with other men if money is involve, or was unable to be aroused by other men unless they watch heterosexual pornography or fantasize about women.[6] Perhaps these men think about economic benefits, but they do not talk about calculations and trading sex for money. Instead, they talk about friendship (*amistad*)—at least in their own cases. Gerson contrasts his own relationship with others who are more concerned with material benefits:

---

6.   Schifter (1998) eventually got around to noting that *cacherismo* has many exceptions, that *cacheros* are actually not as heterosexual as they are represented in San José's popular culture, and that most of the males who rent their bodies in Lila's House have intimate contact at times with the penises of some customers. In this section of Schifter's book about fantasies and pleasures elicited from the *cacheros*, it becomes evident that not only economic need or greed, but also pure pleasure (especially from receiving fellatio) seems to draw *cacheros* into—or at least keep them in—sex work. Watching pornography seems to expand their erotic imaginations. In particular, orgies in which they have sex with both men and women become attractive. The line between homosexuality and heterosexuality blurs as they feel inclined to having sex with both men and women during the orgies. Fantasy affects practice and practice affects fantasy (p. 87). Oral sex with clients becomes one of their favorite practices, a necessary one, indeed. According to Lila, the pleasure of receiving oral sex is what keeps many *cacheros* in the business and will eventually lead them to do "everything" (p. 84).

I: Are there economic benefits or gifts that accrue to men who have relations with homosexuals.

G: In the case of [me and] my partner no. We aid each other. At times when I have a problem with money, he aids me. When I was not working and needed money or some other thing, he helped me....

I: The friends you know who have sex with homosexuals, do they receive economic benefit?

G: Yes. There are some who do it only for money.

I: Yes, Is this common?

G: Yes, it's common. I have some friends, yes, among them it is common.

I: Are some doing it for pleasure or only for money, or a mixture.

G: I don't know if I would say that it is for pleasure, but many believe that everything is for money.

I: So that if they have money they would not be doing it.

G: Right: They wouldn't do it without money. I don't know for sure, but for me, I do it for pleasure and because he is my partner, right?

I: For love.

G: For love. Not for money, for love. I do it for love and because it pleases me to do it but I have friends who do it solely for money.

The closest approach to acknowledging financial calculation was Enrique's speculation about the future: "In the future, I don't think that I will have sexual relations with a homosexual. But keeping the friendship like a brother and a friend, of a homosexual might be a good investment for the future in case I run into economic problems." Even in this statement, friendship remains salient after he imagines sex with a homosexual partner has ceased.

Jaime stressed that sometimes when he goes out with his homosexual partner the partner pays, sometimes Jaime pays, and sometimes they both pay. It seems likely that these men under-reported the extent to which their homosexual partners paid for gifts, meals, entertainment, etc. The *hombres* were in conventionally masculine but not notably well-paid occupations (Gerson was about to join the military; the others were auto mechanics and cab drivers).

"Once broken, never the same": The risk of being penetrated

Enrique told me that a very masculine-appearing friend of his had changed his taste (*gusta*) and began to have those of a homosexual. Although he was very masculine, now he is *gay*.

> I: That's the same as "homosexual?"
> E: Yes.
> I: Why?
> E: Because he developed the taste for being penetrated and that pleased him, then this led to other—other thoughts and to like the ideas of being homosexual. Although he was very masculine, now he is *gay*.
> I: That's the same as "homosexual?"
> E: Yes.

Although Enrique believed that homosexuality is congenital for some, observation led him to conclude that some homosexuals are born and some are made. (As for himself, he said that he "would not consent to being penetrated: it could not happen.")

José shared this belief:

> The majority of homosexuals are born that way, though in certain cases the reason is because of the society. Perhaps if men have a lot of sex with homosexuals, then they become homosexual. Because—here there are two meanings: *culero* is a man, an *activo* who makes love to a *pasivo*, to a homosexual. One could say he is a *culero* because he is one who penetrates asses. The homosexual is the homosexual…. Homosexuals are those who define themselves as homosexuals. A *culero* is someone who likes to have relations with a homosexual.

I: So that you could become a *culero*?

J: Yes.

Usually, *culero* refers to the one whose *culo* is penetrated (the homosexual, the *pasivo*) rather than to the men who like to penetrate *culos*,[7] but for José even someone who is exclusively insertive is in danger of losing his *hombre* status and becoming a homosexual. Rather than enhancing his masculine status, sexual contact with males—even insertive contact—contaminates and endangers it.

Gerson also confirmed homosexuals' belief that, as a true *hombre*, he does not generally like male partners but only his partner, who just happens to be a male. The monogamy of confining oneself to only one male partner appears to cleanse any trace of homosexuality away from the relationship, as well as any risk of disease from unprotected intercourse. When I asked Gerson if he considered himself homosexual, he replied simply: "No, I consider myself simply an *hombre*. I like to have sex, but only with my partner."

Gerson told me that his (younger) brother is a homosexual. Feigning naiveté, I asked how the two brothers were different, since both had sex with males. Gerson replied that his brother was penetrated by men.

INTERVIEWER: And you, have you been penetrated?

GERSON: No, never.... I would not like that.

I: You've never had a fantasy?

G: I've never had one and I believe that I will never spread [my legs for penetration]. Each to his own taste.

I: Do you believe that if you were penetrated you would change and not be an *hombre* any longer?

---

7.   Gerson defined *culero* as a homosexual. Yet a third understanding was advanced by Enrique, though he explicitly said he did not understand the meaning of *culero*, but speculated, "I imagine that it signifies the you have fear of the dark or that you have fear of someone who is bigger than you."

G: I don't know, because I've never had that done to me. I cannot be penetrated. It might change my way of being.

Rather than a concern about the pain of penetration, the fear *hombres* acknowledge is that if they were anally penetrated, they might like it and, then, would have to seek it out, which is to say, become phallus-seeking homosexuals instead of phallus-wielding *hombres*. These men conceive that receptive anal sex might be pleasurable. Indeed, they are witnesses—of their own (homo)sexual partners—of males for whom the desire to be penetrated is so strong that it defines and constitutes them. The belief is that trying it is to hurl oneself into an abyss of debauchery, never to be a man again (or even a serious being—see below).

Other observers (e.g., Brandes 1981:232-34, Prieur 1998:200-02) have claimed that a fear of enjoying being anally penetrated is a salient concern for Latino males. "If I let him fuck me I'd probably like it and then I'd do it again, and then I'd be queer," a young Guatemalteco told Lane (1978:56). For Hermes in the Brazilian writer Caio Abreu's novella "Sergeant Garcia" that fear is realized: "I knew that once it had been awakened, it wouldn't sleep again" (Abreu 1983:277). From Costa Rica, Schifter elicited *chapuline* ("locust," an *activo* hustler-thief) views that

> nobody should let his guard down, because at any moment danger can strike…. [If a man's anus is penetrated,] the organs themselves are transformed and become "homosexualized."
>
> "That queen I screw is dominated by her ass. She has an insatiable faggot ass. She's lost control of her own asshole."
>
> "And yours?" we ask José a locust.
>
> "Mine is a man's ass," he replies proudly. I've trained it only to shit!" (2000:122-23)

Morales (1997) recounted the admonitory Central American story in which "*El arrunido* is a young man who has submitted to anal sex. He is never again the same. Some quality about him has changed. This parallels the virginal status of woman who are defiled if they have sex prior to marriage. The implication is that anal sex is quite dangerous. Like a drug it[s pleasure] is addictive."

Schmitt (1992:8) explained that the danger of coming to find being penetrated desirable, indeed, irresistible is a part of (transcontinental) Islamic cosmology: "To most Muslims anal lust is not really unnatural. One has to avoid getting buggered precisely in order not to acquire a taste for it and thus become addicted. It is like an infectious disease: once infected it is difficult to get rid of it."[8] Such a belief seems to have a circum-Mediterranean diffusion and to have been carried to the New World by Iberian *conquistadores*. Lumsden (1991:45) reports that "there is even a term, *hechizos*, ["made ones"], for former *mayates* [masculine partners of effeminate *pasivos*] who have become complete homosexuals over time, terminating any pretense to having a [female] *novia*."

Jaime also believed that being anally penetrated (even once) would transform who he is, though he suggested it would make him a "bisexual" rather than a "homosexual."

Perhaps because it is so unthinkable that he could be penetrated, Allan seemed more confident than the others that he was immune to being transformed into a homosexual if he were penetrated

> ALLAN [recalling his first homosexual experience}: I was aroused and tried to make it, to have relations with him. It was the first time. I penetrated in his ass, something I had not done before. It hurt a little, for the first time, right? And then it was pleasurable and I had relations with him. But only penetrating homosexuals. Never them penetrating me.

---

8. The anxiety that one may like getting fucked if he tries it parallels the anxiety about one's women (especially wife) getting to like sex and slipping from the Madonna to the *puta* (or, at least, *chingada*) role, a nagging concern of those living by the particularly acute double standard of Latin American culture. Only Santa María was able to be both a mother and a virgin (see LaFaye 1976, W. Taylor 1987, Martin 1990).

I: You put it in them, but they never put it in you?

A: Yes, exactly.

I: What do you think would happen if your anus was penetrated?

A: No. It would not make me feel good, because I know that I am a man and would not like someone doing that to me, because I am not a homosexual, I am a man.

Sex with homosexuals, male honor, and social acceptance

Not one of the *hombres* indicated that he bragged to other *hombres* about penetrating homosexuals or said anything to indicate that doing so enhanced his masculine honor. They were discreet about such relationships, not mentioning them to neighbors, friends, or family members. Not all seemed ashamed of engaging in such behavior (even if solely as an insertor): those deeply ashamed of such behavior would not have agreed to be interviewed about it. However, they all knew that their society regarded **any** involvement as suspect.

> INTERVIEWER: How many men do you know who know you have relations with your partner?
> GERSON: Only the homosexuals who know me that come here, who know the barrio where I live, are the only ones who know. Among my friends, no one knows.
> I: None?
> G: None.
> I: And your family?
> G: Only my [homosexual] brother.... I have always lived alone, not visiting cousins, I don't like to visit my family. I like to live my life.... So they don't know. Nor uncles, nor parents. I've never been open with them.

He also maintains that he does not care what others think:

G: I don't care about the acceptance of society. Because society does not live anyone's life, right? If one does not work, one does not eat. Society is not going to give what I want, right? It will not give pleasure or satisfaction.

I: Do your friends know that you are in a relationship with a homosexual?

G: Some know. It doesn't bother me who knows or doesn't know, because I have to be myself. Both of us protect having the relationship, no?

....

I: When you have experience with a homosexual how do you feel? Do you feel good, guilty, worried?

G: I feel good, because if one is going to have a relationship with a homosexual, one knows what is going to happen, right? and one does not feel penitent about doing that: I have never felt guilty about what I've done.

Nonetheless, he is discreet: "I neither deny nor announce it.... For other people, it is very scandalous, and it might make problems.... Some [friends from the colony in which he lives] know that I come here, but are not certain I have relations. They may suspect, but I don't confirm it."

Jaime showed awareness of the "modern" psychiatric stigmatization of both partners, saying that he would not take any opportunities that presented themselves for other sexual relations with homosexuals "because finding out that a man who likes to have sex with a man, is dishonored, and ipso facto is discharged from the military if it is known.... Those who have sex with *hombres* and those who have sex with gays are equally dishonored."

The only one?

There was great variability in these *hombres'* estimates of the extent to which there are other *hombres* from their neighborhoods (*colonias*) who have sex with homosexuals. Although he said that he had various friends in the city of San Pedro who had homosexual partners, Jaime twice stated that he is the only one who has had sexual experiences with a homosexual. Enrique also said that he was unique in his colony, as did Gerson.

Jaime, on the other hand, estimated that half the men he knows have penetrated a homosexual. When I asked how he knew this, he replied: "I've seen. I know the class of persons. Because I have experience in the gay *ambiente*, I have seen them, and know well who is an *hombre*, so that it can happen. In my colony, half have penetrated other men, There are various gays there."

Hombres' conceptions of homosexuality

Even in a sample of seven men, there is considerable difference in the elaboration of differing species of sexuality, though the primary dichotomizations are the same for all.

At the level of natal/biological sex, there is consensus that homosexuals are males, not women trapped in male bodies or a third sex. It is in the sense of biological sex that these *hombres* refer to homosexuals of incomplete masculinity as "*hombres.*"

The simplest model of differentiation within biological males is a simple one of sexuality in which there are *hombres* (penetrating males) and *homosexuales* (penetrated males). Gender is consistent with sexual role, but "what you are is determined by what you do" (Fausto).

Freddie said that the only difference between *hombres* and homosexuals is that homosexuals are penetrated and they see themselves as or believe they are women. I asked Freddie what are some differences between an *hombre* and a homosexual. He said: (1) One can only be *hombre* or homosexual; (2) an *hombre* is a macho; homosexuals, on the other hand, say: "Ay, no" (a "feminine" interjection); (3) homosexuals wear *calzones* (female underwear), *hombres* wear *calzoncillos* (male underwear).

José asserted that the direction of penetration is the sole difference between a homosexual and a man. He said that he could recognize some homosexuals on the street, but that there are also homosexuals who do not appear to be homosexual.

Gerson also suggested seeking and liking relations with an *hombre* as the basis for distinguishing *hombres* and homosexuals:

> I: You also have relations with men but you are not homosexual. Why is he [Gerson's brother] homosexual?
> G: Perhaps because he likes it, no? To have relations.
> I: But are you then also homosexual?
> G: Homosexual in the partners and in the sense that I like to have relations with homosexuals. You could say that I am homosexual in that sense.
> I: Or bisexual because you have relations with women and with men.
> G: I don't know what to call that.

After he asserted that his brother is "like me, but he has some effeminate aspects, like crying when he is hit," Gerson said that not only had he been told that his brother was homosexual, but he had seen him being penetrated, and has talked to his brother's *hombre* partner on the phone. We continued with Gerson making a categorical differentiation based on penetration, and being puzzled by my only-somewhat hypothetical question about someone masculine who liked to be penetrated:

> I: You believe that there is a difference between you and your brother who is homosexual and that you are different.
> G: The difference is that he likes to be penetrated: this is the difference between me and homosexuals. And, for me, I am not homosexual because I do not like being penetrated. I like to penetrate.
> I: So, if a person is masculine and likes to be penetrated that makes him a homosexual even if he is masculine? Or is there a difference.
> G: There's a difference.
> I: What?

G: If the homosexual partner also is masculine, I don't know. He could not find a masculine one with whom to have relations. Those who are masculine like to penetrate the homosexual, all masculine ones enjoy the pleasure [of penetrating].

Although he asserted the masculinity of his homosexual brother, the category of a masculine male wanting to be penetrated seems unthinkable. However, it is not entirely counterfactual a hypothetical for him. In addition to his homosexual brother, he knows that some homosexuals are married to women and have sired children:

G: My criterion is that the homosexual is the one who initiates it, no? Because no *hombre* is going to want to be homosexual. Because each who is a homosexual has an instinct for that, no? If one is homosexual and likes men, then the man likes the homosexual and the two can have relations. And he is made also not to like women. Some homosexuals do not like women, according to what I know. I don't know what relations they could have, between homosexuals and women.
I: And in the case of heterosexuals, always they like women?
G: Some [of those I know] have some friends who are married and have children and are homosexuals. And they are with women.

For Jaime, there is a third sexuality, and fuzzier gender correlates. In this conception, there are *hombres* who only penetrate (male as well as female orifices), bisexuals who penetrate females and are penetrated by *hombres*, and homosexuals (also called "gays") who are penetrated by *hombres*.

INTERVIEWER: How do you see yourself?
JAIME: I like women. And at the same time I can have sexual relations with a man.
I: But you do not consider yourself gay?
J: No, I do not consider myself gay.
I: Why?
J: Because I am not penetrated.

I: So, the "gay" is the one who is penetrated?

J: I believe that is so. The gay is penetrated.

I: And if you were penetrated, would you be "gay" then?

J: I believe that I would be bisexual, because I like women.

I: "Bisexual" is someone—

J:—who is pleased by women and by men, but the aspect of being pleased by men is that the man make love to him, penetrates him. Then one is a bisexual who likes to penetrate women and who is penetrated by a man.... The gay only is penetrated by a man. Perhaps, the (reason the) gay is not considered an *hombre* is that if a man has sex with a gay he feels like a man. The difference is that if the man is penetrated, that signifies that he has sex with another *hombre*, not with a gay, is going to penetrate for this, this makes the man lose his status of *hombre* and fall into that of bisexual and has sex with a man as in contrast to having sex with a woman. To kiss a man, to have feelings more for a man.

I: And the difference between an *hombre* and a bisexual is that an *hombre* also penetrates women, like the bisexual, but is not penetrated by other men?

J: Yes. He is not penetrated by men. He only penetrates women.

....

I am not penetrated by men. If I was going to be penetrated by a man, I would be bisexual, because I like to penetrate women....

I consider myself all man. (*Me considero todo un hombre.*)

I: And what is the difference between a person like you and an *hombre* who never has had sex with another man? Is there some difference?

J: No. No difference.[9]

---

9.   Jaime suggested *hombre-hombre* for a male who is never penetrated, but not as distinguishing between the biological sex of those whom the *hombre-hombre* penetrates. The ellipsis after the hypothetical bisexuality is a puzzling "But if I only penetrated women, and at times penetrated a man, but was not penetrated by the man, then I am a *transsexual*."

....

> I: Apart from the gay being penetrated and touching the genitals of another man, are there other differences between a *gay* and a *hombre*?
>
> J: Yes. The gay is in love with a man like he is a woman [is with] a normal man. And the man is not in love like the gay.

Jaime opined that to show sexual desire is to become unserious (and, thereby, unworthy of respect): "Seriousness is lost if one is attracted to a man .... *Hombres* never lose their seriousness." When, late in the interview, he flirtatiously said "I would turn to look at you if I saw you in the street," I repeated his statement about showing desire compromising one's masculine seriousness. He smiled and said, "I could lose my seriousness if I liked, if I wanted to." I think that he meant that it was his prerogative to flout convention. Alternatively, as long as it is desire to penetrate, desiring a male is not a very serious offense against masculine status.

Allan suggested "bisexual" for someone who has relations with a homosexual, presumably penetrating the homosexual. In addition to this different conception of "bisexual," Allan volunteered the possibility that homosexuals might have sexual relations with other homosexuals:

> I: How do you know that someone is homosexual.
>
> A: At times it is not clear (that someone is homosexual), but in truth one notes in the person's manner of speaking, also in the movements the person makes, gestures that are not those of a man, right?.... From the annoying, inappropriate questions that are made.... And from having sex.
>
> I: And the homosexuals have sex with whom?
>
> A: With *hombres*.
>
> I: With *hombres*.
>
> A: At times, I believe, though I don't really know, that they might be with other homosexuals, also.

For Gerson, there is further distinction by gender among homosexuals of effeminate (prototypically *travestis*) and (socially passable) masculine. I have already quoted statements of relief that an *hombre*'s own partner is not obviously effeminate.

Although stressing gender as criterial for recognizing homosexuals, Gerson distinguishes *travesti* from non-*travesti* homosexuals:

> I: Can you distinguish a homosexual on the street?
>
> G: Yes.
>
> I: How?
>
> G: Perhaps the gestures, from the mode of speaking, and the signs they make with their facial expressions. I am accustomed to the *ambiente*, so, because of that I know who is *ambiente*, all the gestures that are made, the *musarañas* that are made.
>
> I: What is "musaraña"?
>
> G: The gestures that are made when speaking, that have, that move loosely, they move the mouth to one side, gesture with their hands, things like that.
>
> I: And what is "maneramientos"?
>
> G: Speaking in a woman's voice. Looking like women, *travestis*.
>
> I: Are their homosexuals who are not like that or are all like that?
>
> G: Not all are like that. There are some who look like men, who do not want to be *travestis*: there are all modes of homosexuals. Both the homosexuals and the *travestis* have distinct ways of thinking, no?

Enrique also recounted having been mistaken about someone, attesting that gender appearance is not always consonant with sexual orientation

> I: How do you distinguish *un hombre*? How do you know that a man is *un hombre*?
>
> E: His voice and his manner of speaking distinguish an *hombre*. At times a homosexual can speak like a normal man but has a look at times when you see him only a person who believes that he is a

man, eh, at times, at times you can tell where he begins to declare himself a homosexual man. At times no one can distinguish, but at others.—[especially when] he wants to have sexual relations [it is clear].

....

I: But do you believe that there is some difference between what a man does in bed and what a homosexual does in bed, or do they do the same?

E: I believe that they do the same.

I: Do you believe that there are *hombres* who are penetrated and homosexuals who penetrate.

E: I would say yes, that there are also *hombres* who like to be penetrated.

I: And homosexuals who penetrate.

E: I'd say no on this point.

....

I: You have never seen a homosexual who has sex with homosexuals.

E: No, to my knowledge, no.

That is, there are secret homosexuals, apparent *hombres* who are penetrated, but not homosexuals who are tops (penetrate).

It is also interesting that none of the *hombres* ever referred to homosexuals as *locas*. Indeed, the only time a form of the word was used, it was adjectival rather than nominal, and in the masculine grammatical gender: *loco*, not *loca* (Jaime talking about the gay being crazed with desire for men and takes initiative to secure sex with men, whereas men are indifferent to having sex with gays).

Speculating about future relationships

José also relied upon "the one who wants it is the homosexual" social logic that more or less requires that *hombres* deny desire to do something that they regularly do:

I: A man could never desire (*gustar*) another man?

JOSÉ: No, Never. Homosexuals like men, and if a homosexual likes a man, it is possible for the man to like the homosexual.

I: Has there been a time when you desired a homosexual?

J: No.

I: So they (homosexuals with whom he has had sex) seduced you?

J: In principal, yes. But always with my consent.

I: And why did you do it?

J: First, to experiment like that.

I: But it gave you pleasure?

J: Yes, yes.

I: And do you think that you would undertake a liaison with a homosexual in the future, if presented the opportunity.

J:I don't know. I couldn't answer this question. [A month later he was in a relationship with a homosexual man.]

Jaime said that he looked on his partner

as the unique person who could like and appreciate me very much. Why? I do not believe that I could have a relationship with a gay for my whole life. because my mentality is different and my life will be different than it is at the present time....

I: And what happens if you know another gay and he becomes a partner. Do you believe that you could be all your life with him.

JAIME: I don't know. It would depend, I believe, on how things turn up in starting another new life and knowing another person. I believe that it is the person, not the class of person, that matters, because if he is not a person whose ways I find agreeable, I could never start (a relationship) like that....

For me it is basic to have children, before I reach old age. I do not think I will always be a youth....

[Re adoption:] In this country I believe that the law prohibits it...and single man adopting is also a legal problem.

While expecting that he would abandon homosex, Gerson displayed a more "que será, será" attitude:

GERSON: I like to have relations with both—always protected.
I: You think that you can maintain this lifestyle for ever, for all your life, or do you think you will change?
G: Generally, one thinks it will change, no? But I have not arrived at this extreme of [having to make] a formal decision about [my] life, of deciding to have relations only with my woman or with my [homosexual] partner. I have not been faced with the need to choose one of the two.

....

I think that I will marry, but not now.
I: When?
G: I don't know, perhaps soon, when I reach 25, because I have to see more of life and do more things, right? to be able to decide. I might marry and have children.

7

HOW HOMBRES ADVERTISE

Sometimes an entire sexual career is built around performing phallic work on sexually receptive homosexuals. The penetrator reinforces his role as the one who is in control by charging money for becoming involved sexually. Such an *hombre* also maintains at least the appearance of having less interest in sex with the *loca* than the *loca* has in having sex with him and less interest than the *loca* has in sustaining a relationship (the power of the least interest). As Schifter and Aggleton (1999:154) put it, "The line that divides sexual commerce from homosexuality [implicating the *hombre*] is very thin," and often requires not only official denial but active suppression of coming to enjoy 'work' too much and emotional attachments to those providing both physical pleasure and material benefits to lower-class youths (144-48).

Phallic commerce

Although minimizing the genuine poverty of males who penetrate homosexuals in Brazil, Patrick Larvie's interpretation of statements such as "Of course I'm not a prostitute, but I expect the man to pay for my expenses" can be generalized to Honduras:

> The idea of sex for money provides the context—but does not constitute the principal objective—for sexual relations between many of the *michês* we interviewed and other men. In this way, sex work operates as an institution that provides a ritualized exchange (mate-

rial or symbolic payment) that justifies otherwise stigmatizing sex
acts. (1999:168)

Payment can be interpreted as "saving" an *hombre*'s honor by showing that he is not actually interested in the sex with males: so that he
can tell himself and anyone else who finds about his conduct that he is
not "homosexual," that he is only fucking the *loca* for the money. This
rationale is probably becoming more important, because, in recent
decades, increasing numbers of people are beginning to equate homosexual behavior with being homosexual. The growing and aggressively
proselytizing Protestant churches' drastic and homophobic condemnation of people who engage in homosexual behavior is raising
homophobia to previously unknown degrees across Latin America,
especially in the poorest strata. The diffusion of "modern gay" conceptions in which role dichotomization is not necessarily maintained and
both insertors and insertees are "gay" also increases the pressure felt by
some to claim they are only involved for material gain (not for their
own pleasure), and are not homosexual, even if they are having sex only
with males.

Although not a local interpretation of which I ever encountered
even a hint, one might imagine that payment could work negatively by
threatening *hombres'* honor. Payment might show *locas'* control and
superiority, since *locas* are the ones who have the money to pay *hombres*, and *locas* bend *hombres'* will by the power of their money. Payment for sex could also spoil *hombres'* honor by equating them with
prostitutes, who have a low social status and are stigmatized. This
interpretation was not made even by those whose self-esteem might be
enhanced by it (that is, not even one of the *locas* with whom I talked).

Most likely, payment creates an image of *hombres* ripping off *locas*,
which works to further stigmatize *locas* as destined to be exploited and
enhances males' masculinity as taking whatever they want. The most
intriguing question is why *locas* do not just accept, but positively
embrace, a system in which they pay for being abjected and do not use
their economic advantage to call a tune other than the one in which

hombres "get off" both in the sense of ejaculation and that of going their own way, leaving the homosexual partners who support them for female partners whom they must support.[1]

The pose of lacking interest

In this book's prelude, I described my initial encounter with the expectation that the homosexual should pay for sex with an *hombre* mentioned in the book's prelude. Early in my 1997 fieldwork I had an especially vivid experience with an *hombre* who illustrated *hombre* attempts not to show too much desire. Although he was obviously interested in having a sexual adventure with me, the young man conspicuously avoided taking any initiative.

The story began on Tuesday, November 4, 1997 when I was sitting on the stairs of Centro Cultural Sampedrano, waiting for the library to open. It was around 1:00 PM. I saw a man in his mid-twenties walking up the street. He was wearing a tank-top and his arms looked rather muscular, so I thought he was going to the gym up the street. His walk was slightly effeminate or, at least, not as masculine as most young *hombres* of his age.

As he approached, he looked at me with "eyes-of-desire." I put it all together and figured out that he was *de ambiente*. He asked someone else where the library was while repeatedly establishing eye-contact with me. I approached him and explained where the library was. We began chatting. His name was Héctor M. He had come to the library to do some homework for his sister. He told me he had been in San

---

1. I had no indication of anything resembling the phenomenon among the male prostitutes in Lila's House (Schifter 1998), whose need for money to buy drugs dissolved the "I'm exclusively a penetrator" posture. Although the view from outside is one of exploitation of *locas,* this is not the view of the latter. *Locas* would never admit having little control. They say that they pay and they have all the control of the situation, and portray *hombres* as silly, as people easy to manipulate.

Pedro only for about a month. He had spent the previous years in Tegucigalpa, although he was born and raised in Arenal, Yoro.

When the library opened, we went in. Héctor was helped by the librarian. I went to the restroom. As I was urinating, I heard someone enter. After a few seconds, I turned around to see Héctor standing behind me and staring at me. I said "hi" and continued. Then he went to the urinals and also urinated. I could see his penis but I did not see him looking at mine. We chatted a little in the restroom. Then I began brushing my teeth. The librarian also came to the restroom and began brushing his teeth. Héctor left the restroom. When I entered the main library's room again, I saw Héctor was sitting in the middle of the large, rectangular room. He saw me and winked at me. By then, I was totally positive that he was in the *ambiente.* Straight young guys who are not into being *buitres* do not wink at other guys, though *buitres* may. Héctor, however, did not look like a *buitre* but, rather, struck me as a *solapa. Buitres* usually dress expensively, are extremely masculine in demeanor, and the way they look at a homosexual is rather mean and greedy instead of the lustful glances that Héctor was giving me.

I did not stop at his table. I sat at the end of the room but stared at Héctor. Every few minutes Héctor would look at me and I would smile back at him. He would not smile but maintained a neutral look. Then he walked to the photocopy machine with the librarian. To do that he had to walk closer to my table. He looked at me when he passed, and I smiled more openly. I think this time he smiled back at me.

After he finished with the photocopies he came and sat at my table. We chatted for about an hour and a half. He told me that he was not doing "anything" at this time in San Pedro. He was looking for a job, but he was taking it very easily—no rush. He was helping in his home. He was 26 years old, had not finished elementary school, and had been working for the past two years as a clerk for a government office.

Héctor told me that from the very first time he saw me he thought I was from the US. He thought I did not speak Spanish. That was the reason he did not talk to me—until I addressed him in Spanish. When

I told him that I had been living in the US for the previous seven years, he confided me that his dream was to go to the US so he could feel more free and have more work opportunities and larger horizons. He asked me if I could help him to move to the US. I told him I would do what I could, but I immediately told him that there was not much I could offer to him, besides giving him some contact information.

Then he started talking about famous women, such as Princess Diana, Jacqueline Kennedy Onassis, Marilyn Monroe, Madonna, etc., saying how much he admired them, etc. The conversation was getting exceptionally boring to me. He was talking about all these beautiful women and how much he admired them. I was expecting a speech next about beauty pageants and the Venezuelan Miss Universe, but luckily, his rambling monologue did not go there. I just could not picture a heterosexual Honduran man talking about female actresses and models instead of soccer games! I thought that he must be gay, that is, a queen.

I do not remember how he raised the issue of HIV. He said that a couple of weeks previously he tested for the HIV and the results were negative. He had to test because of a job for which he was applying. Then we talked a little bit about safe sex, using a condom, etc.

The chemistry between us seemed good and I felt we were raising lots of steam. We would stare at each other and smile coquettishly. He was shaking his legs and body while talking. He almost looked like he was mounting someone. At some point I thought that if he continued rubbing his crotch with that movement, he was going to have an orgasm. I, then, suggested going to have a drink somewhere else. He agreed. I stood up and went to the desk to reclaim my backpack. He remained seated for a minute before standing up (waiting for his erection to subside, I believe).

We went to a coffee-shop since he wanted to have coffee. At the library he made it clear that he only had money for the bus ride back home, so I invited him for the cup of coffee. At the coffee shop, he made his sexual interests clear. He said that a woman from the US, a friend of his in Tegucigalpa, had once kissed him in the mouth and it felt good. Then I asked him about other experiences. He said that he did not have sex with that *gringa*—she was not attractive enough for him; she was too old for him (in her 40s), and too fat. He told me about a girlfriend he had in Tegucigalpa, just before moving to San Pedro. He said she was very horny and described some sex scenes to me. They had sex on several occasions. She was older than him and paid him and gave gifts to him (*a buitre* profile showing, possibly transforming a *loca* into a real woman who paid for his stud services).

As he was talking, an attractive young woman entered the coffee-shop. He looked with heated eyes at her, and made a remark about how sexy she was. Then he looked at another woman and said he liked to look at women's butts. Before this, he had not been looking at women in such a predatory *hombre* manner. I began to feel a bit inse-cure about my inference that he was a *solapa*, and asked him directly if he had ever had sexual experiences with men. His face turned somber and serious. He said something like, "Well, since you asked me that question, I will tell you the truth: yes, I've had encounters with two homosexuals." (I found strange that, as it had happened in other occa-sions as well, a Honduran man confesses to me that he has had sex with *two* and only *two* homosexuals, as if *two* is the maximum acceptable number of homosexual encounters for a Honduran straight man to have. Moreover, the person speaking is never homosexual; only the persons with whom he had sex are.)

He told me the stories of his homosexual experiences. Both experi-ences had occurred in the preceding year (in Tegucigalpa), the last one about six months earlier. (I wondered if it was a coincidence that he took the HIV test exactly six months after his last homosexual encoun-ter, considering that six months is the accepted window period for antibodies for HIV to appear)

In his "first" experience he was in a *colectivo* (a sort of taxi that is shared by several people and follows a fixed route) at night with only one other passenger. They were both seated on the back seat. "Sud-denly"—he claimed—(but I was sure that Héctor gave the other passenger plenty of lustful eye-contact, just as he did me), the other passenger began rubbing one of Héctor's thighs. Héctor liked it and got aroused. The guy apparently rubbed Héctor's crotch in the dark of the back seat and noticed Héctor's arousal. Héctor gave the man his telephone number, but the man never called.

The second man Héctor "met" was more responsive and they met more than once. As in the other case, Héctor gave the man his telephone number, so the man called Héctor each time he wanted to see him. Héctor and the man would go to the cinema, the man would caress Héctor's thighs and crotch, get him aroused and finally pull Héctor's penis out of his pants and fellate him. On the last occasion they met, the man brought Héctor to a dark, unknown, and sleazy bar with mirrors on its walls. The place was almost empty. They went to a dark corner and the man got Héctor aroused again. After fellating Héctor, the man put a condom on Héctor's penis and sat on it. Héctor fucked the man while sitting in the bar. Héctor just sat with a full erection while the man rode him. The fantasy of the man was to look at this scene in the mirror. Héctor reached orgasm quickly, and apparently nobody noticed anything. The man did not call Héctor again after that. (That Héctor was able to become erect and to reach climax again after his first ejaculation shows desire in an objective sense, though this is clearly not his interpretation of his story.)

In both cases, especially the second one, it was clear that Héctor was playing the role of the desired (young and attractive) *hombre*. Héctor never touched (at least in his account)—he was touched. He never gave oral sex—he was given it. He did not even fuck—the man sat on his penis and rode him. Whether this is true or not I do not know. How Héctor chose to portray himself and his history of sexual contact with males was more interesting to me than his actual behavior. I would have liked to know what he actually did, how he reacted, but could only gain access to his version of his earlier encounters.

However, I was able to observe his behavior with me. I asked him if he would like to have sex with me. He looked shocked. Had he not been expecting anything like this coming from me? Certainly he was not shocked because of the disclosure of my desire, since, as he later told me, he had realized that I was attracted to him from the very first time he saw me, because of the way I was looking, staring, and smiling at him. Was I being too direct then? Was connecting something that could be done but never spoken about?

He said "no" and then remained silent He seemed to be thinking lots of things. I asked him what he was thinking about. He said he was feeling lots of fear. Fear about what, I asked, but he would not reply.

Then it occurred to me that my perception of him being a *solapa* was because of his body language, which was clearly sending me signals that he was interested in me (and that he was homosexual). Maybe Héctor was in denial of his homosexual desires. Or perhaps he was consciously taking on the role of the *buitre* for psychological or economic reasons.

Although he deceived me with his lustful eyes, his effeminate manners, his topics of discussion, and his humble dress, that he was classifiable as a *buitre* was confirmed when he told me that from the very beginning of our encounter he noticed that I was looking at him with desire. (Was he aware that he too was looking at me with desire, I wondered?) Maybe his desires were my dollars and a direct plane ticket to the US rather than my looks or sex appeal (see Morton 1995, Murray 1996b). Or most likely, all of the above combined.

The fact that I was inviting him for a coffee and later to the cinema (where he suggested I could touch him), and that he showed no active desire toward me, and took no initiative, but rather merely permitted mine, also reaffirmed his status as a *buitre*.

Other *buitres* I met in Honduras behaved in a similar way: they would not take any initiative that might seem to show sexual desire on their part. Instead, they (passively!) made themselves available to the sexual advances of the. Nevertheless, for the homosexual to satisfy their sexual urges and reach the *hombre*'s body, the homosexual had to pay by inviting the *hombre* for drinks, food, and to the cinema, among other things.

After leaving the coffee shop, we went to "Cinema 1," but Héctor was not admitted because he was wearing a tank-top. The rejection recurred in Cinemas 2 and 3. Héctor suggested that I could buy a shirt for him so he could enter a cinema. This *buitre* was getting more and more expensive, I thought! How long would I have to be paying before he realizes that he actually likes me, I wondered (to myself).

We could not find a cheap shirt. Only then he remembered that he had a cousin living in the same neighborhood. After about ten minutes, he returned wearing a black t-shirt. Upon Héctor's suggestion, we went to see a film about a man who turns into a woman (a favorite topic for Honduran *locas* but not for Honduran *hombres*, I must say). Héctor was very enthusiastic about seeing the film.

I paid for the movie tickets (L. 50 total, about two US dollars for each ticket) and bought a big cup of coke and popcorn for him. I bought *nachos* with melted cheese for myself. During the film, Héctor talked to me in a flirtatious way and would look seductively at me, almost as if supplicating me to touch him. I, however, decided on an experiment: I told him that I was going to respect him, and that I was going to wait for him to touch me first. Checking my hypothesis about *hombres* taking a passive attitude toward homosexual's sexual advances, I said that I would not touch him until he touched me.

He said "no," that it was not right. Well, now it was a challenge, I thought: who will "fall" first. By this time I was melting for him, and this challenge helped me restore my integrity and feel less frustrated at the excruciatingly slow pace of our conjunction.

At some point during the film I noticed he was playing with himself. Then he rubbed my thigh with his knee (not with his hand) in such a way that he could claim it was an accident—or like his body was taking over without his authorization. A hand touching my body would have been a sign of too much eagerness. The way he touched me with his knee was by thrusting his knee below my thigh and raising my thigh a bit. I whispered to him: "Touch me!" but he refused.

After the film, as we were walking down the street, he asked me why I did not touch him during the film, almost as if reprimanding me. I said that I was waiting for him to touch me first. He said that it was not right, that I was supposed to touch him first. Had I been a woman, would you have touched me first, I asked? "Of course I would," he said. But because I was not a woman but a homosexual, I was supposed to make the move. because he was the *hombre* and I was the homosexual. As an *hombre*, he could not possibly be interested in initiating anything with another male.

We said good bye and agreed I was going to call him the next morning. When I called him the next morning we agreed to meet later at the library of the Centro Cultural Sampedrano, the place we first met. He did not show up, and I never saw him again.

Territoriality, appearances of helplessness, and danger

Charging for sex is not always performed in subtle ways. Sometimes it is done by force, as in robberies. Sometimes an *hombre* feels that he deserves payment from a *loca* even without any delivery to the *loca* of the *hombre*'s phallus having occurred. The mere difference in social status separating the *loca* from the *hombre* justifies (in the view of some *hombres*, and even of some *locas*) the *hombre* in charging or beating the *loca* if the *loca* enters his territory. As the incident related below shows, the fee that the *hombre* requires of the *loca* for being in his presence, in the world of "real men," is like paying a toll.

On an October 1997 Saturday, Osvaldo and I went to meet Fausto in his barrio, the El Roble colony. We wanted to go to "*el bordo*" (the border of the river and of the colony) and the river, Armenta. Fausto, known in his barrio to be homosexual, was waiting for us by the bus stop. A few meters away there was a group of workers resting with their shovels under the shade of some trees, their "territory." One of them, Mario, charged me a toll; he asked me for my sunglasses. I just smiled. We chatted for a while. Then he asked for my sunglasses again, but I said "no" and smiled, keeping the interaction at the joking level.

We then went to the barrio's cantina, a shack constructed of wood and tin. Fausto told me that that man who was asking me for the sunglasses is a delinquent, that he robs people by the river, but that he would not do anything to us, because he was friendly with Fausto.

About ten of the men, all in their early 20s, left the shade and followed us into the cantina. At first, they—especially the youngest-looking one—teased each other. He would suggestively touch one of the increasingly drunken older men. The older man would chase and swing at him with a shovel, but the young guy who was not drunk would run away, evading the shovel attack to the amusement of the crowd. This young man and another young man also were dancing in a sensual manner to the Caribbean music that was playing.

Fausto told me that all this display of dancing and horseplay was not "normal" in a drinking environment like this. Fausto thought that the men were becoming excited because of our presence. They were not looking directly at us—at least not at this point. After about twenty minutes, four of them began getting closer and closer to us, until they finally joined us by sitting at the same table. This happened gradually as Fausto began introducing them one by one to me and by quietly telling me that he had had sex with two of them.

After we were seated together, Fausto explained that I was doing fieldwork on homosexuality. This opened the door for me to ask them questions about their perceptions of gender and sexuality. This setting had the advantage that people were relaxed and semi-inebriated so that they felt less embarrassment than would usually be the case in talking about these matters. On the other hand, the fact that every answer was heard by the rest of their peers created pressure and invariably influenced the veracity of answers that were personally/emotionally compromising. Finally, the fact that we were in their territory, and furthermore that we were *locas* in an *hombre* territory, made us vulnerable, and probably increased their braggadocio.

The youngest-looking man, whom I will call Rivereño (one who lives by the river), told me he was 20 years old. He said that he has lived with two *maricas* ("sissies"), one in Mexico, and one in Honduras. Rivereño claimed that the Bible said that it is not right for two men to have sex and that he did it because of financial necessity. He said he only lived a couple of days with each. He said one *marica* was 25 and the other around 27. He was age 17 in the first case (in Mexico) and a year or so older in the second. He said that he expects that by the time he reaches age thirty he will have done it with about thirty *maricas*.

I wondered in a loud stage whisper if he had not already done it with thirty *maricas*. Everyone laughed and he reddened as if caught in a lie. Fausto had already told me that he had had sex with him; and that the guy had a large penis. Rivereño proceeded to show me with a stick how long his penis was. He said it was the length of a palm plus a bit more (about 8.5 inches).

Fausto said I was homosexual and that I wanted to have sex with him. Rivereño asked how much I was going to pay him. I told him that I do not like to pay the person I have sex with, that I like to have sex with people for pleasure only, and that I enjoy knowing that the other person is with me because he desires me and not my money. Rivereño said he would have sex with me for the pleasure of it then. He said he liked to be fellated. He asked me if I liked to fellate. I told him not really, unless I knew we later were going to have anal intercourse. He did not look very enthusiastic about having anal intercourse. He told me that he has a woman, that he is very horny, and that he can fuck seven times in a row.

All this conversation was public. The people at the table were listening to it, adding comments, and enjoying it. I also think they were getting aroused. Most of them had either drunk some alcohol or smoked some marijuana prior to the conversation.

A man in his late thirties wearing shorts and no shirt was sitting by my side. He repeatedly—though sporadically—rubbed his leg against mine and grabbed my hand, the side of my torso, and what he could of my buttocks (I was sitting). It was subtle enough that it did not bother me or distract my attention from the conversation. The man was quite drunk, however, and added his nonsensical comments on several occasions. No one seemed to pay attention to him (this was the same man who had chased Rivereño away with his shovel). I ignored his pawings, trying to get as much information as I could from my conversation with Rivereño.

I asked another young man about his sexual experiences with other men. His name was Eduardo and he was wearing a baseball cap. His eyes were quite red; he looked like he was high on marijuana. He said he was 23 years old. Unlike Rivereño, who looked sober, more greedy, and astute and experienced in negotiating sex in exchange for money, Eduardo looked more innocent. He looked angelic, and smiled frequently. He seemed shy, and I imagine it would have been hard for him to open up on this type of topic had he not been high on something.

He showed interest in me from the very beginning. He would stare at me and smile a lot. He was sitting close to me, almost waiting for his turn to interact with me. He seemed ecstatic when I directed my attention to him. He told me that he has never had an experience with another man, but that he was willing to have his first one (he would smile and look with dilated pupils, while saying this, so I imagined that he wanted to have his "first experience" with me). Eduardo was the young man who had been dancing with Rivereño earlier on. Eduardo looked a little bit embarrassed telling me all this in front of his friends, but at the same time he looked excited about it.

During the conversation with the two boys, more young men slid over. One was known as "El Turco" (the Turk) because of his big nose. He was the most forward of the three. He also looked like he was high on marijuana. He would stare lustily at me as I was talking to the other men. He would whisper things to me like "I want to have your ass" and "I want you badly" as I was talking to the other boys. I felt El Turco was a little pushy and mostly ignored him. El Turco seemed more experienced in dealing with situations like this than some of his companions and it was clear that he wanted some reward for his sexual services. He repeatedly asked me to invite him to have a beer; a thing that I refused to do each time, by claiming that I was not carrying any money on me (this was the same explanation I gave to the 20-year old Rivereño when he asked for financial rewards for sexual services). Men asked what I had in my *mariquera* (a waist bag I was carrying). They asked if I had money there. I said no.

Fausto told me that he had had sex with El Turco on many occasions. El Turco struck me as being a "professional" *buitre*. I also learned that El Turco was the leader of the local *mara* or youth gang. El Turco's arousal struck me as fake, not genuine like Eduardo's, or even Rivereño's. I asked El Turco how old he was and he said 22. I asked him if he had had sex with another man and he said that he had with two men. I found it amusing that again the answer was the recurrent "two." El Turco later confessed to having fucked many *locas*, confirming my suspicion that he was quite experienced at this type of interaction and was a "professional" *buitre*.

I asked the guys who claimed to have had experiences with men what a *marica* has that a woman does not. Rivereño said nothing, except that he gets paid in the first case. He then added that he liked the pleasure of being fellated, and that many women did not like to do that. El Turco said that men's asses feel great because they are more *socado* (tight) than vaginas. Then I wondered, since I have heard that comment before, why these *hombres* do not then fuck women in the ass. But El Turco, almost guessing my next question, added that the *culo* ("ass") of *maricas* was tighter than the *culo* of women (implying that he has fucked both), because *maricas* knew how to squeeze the penis once inside. (I believe this argument to be true as I have been told by *locas* how they had learned to squeeze their anuses to make *hombres* more excited.) This seemed to amuse the audience, who appeared to get more and more excited. Even Mario, the delinquent, other people from the *mara*, the bartender, and the neighborhood guard (a private security watchman) joined the conversation. At this point probably a group of about 15 men were surrounding us in a tight circle. Such an event is very unlikely to occur in a straight bar in the US. But in Honduras all these neighborhood working class *hombres*, many of them with shovels in their hands, were surrounding us, amazed at the conversation and visibly getting more and more excited and aroused.

El Turco was the most persistent of the group, wanting to go to the river "and have an orgy." Everyone seemed excited by the idea. I told Fausto that I was afraid of going to the river with so many drunken men. I was afraid of being gang-raped. Osvaldo was terrified and did not say a word during the whole conversation. Unusually, this time it was not Osvaldo, but me who was the center of attention and desire, perhaps because I was very public in asking questions about sex. However, it was not clear to me the extent to which their desire to sexually possess my body was intertwined with desires to possess my apparent wealth (my sunglasses, my *mariquera* and anything of value (money?) that could have been inside it), my perceived higher status and education, or my lighter skin, hair, and foreign looks. Osvaldo, on the other hand, even though he was a *marica*—and a feminine looking one—was not exotic. He was still one of them and did not seem to have anything of value on him. My friendliness also contrasted with Osvaldo's aloofness.

Then Fausto and I left the cantina and headed to the river. Despite the fear, my curiosity to see what these *hombres* would do was greater. I also trusted Fausto's judgment. Osvaldo said he was not going to go. He left, going straight to the bus stop, where he quickly took the first bus back home. Osvaldo did not tell me what was going on, but he later told me that in the past he had gone with Fausto to this river and the same men had tried to gang-rape him. That time he escaped by telling them that he was going to the cantina to buy some drinks and bring them to the riverside. Osvaldo also told me later that he over-heard some guys saying that since we did not buy them drinks at the cantina, they were going to *ponerla* (to put a knife to someone, mean-ing to rob us).

As we were walking down the road toward the river I saw that a gang composed of about five guys, including Rivereño and El Turco, also going to the river. I told Fausto that there were too many of them, that the situation could easily get out of control. Fausto tried to talk to them, but they took off into the bushes. I told Fausto that I did not want to go to the river, that the situation looked too dangerous. Fausto, who by this time was quite drunk himself, insisted that every-thing was fine, the gang were all his friends, and he and they lived in the same neighborhood. As we were discussing whether or not to go into the bushes toward the river, Mario, the delinquent, and another guy who was also in the cantina, approached us, smiling enticingly. When they were really close to us, Mario's partner's face turned angry or serious and he tried to grab my sunglasses as he said: "Give me those sunglasses." I resisted. Fausto stepped in front of me and said some-thing like, "Come on, what's going on?!" Mario attacked Fausto with his shovel (but he did not hit him) and looking very stern and said something to the effect of "Don't you interfere!"

Remembering that Mario was a professional delinquent who usually carries a knife to attack his victims, I was afraid that the situation could escalate dangerously into a bloody attack. Every time I went to the river I was prepared for the worst (I was told countless times that it is very common to be mugged by the river), thus I calculated that I was not carrying more than ten dollars' worth on me and that resisting was an unnecessary risk to take. I immediately gave him my sunglasses. Then Mario asked for my mariquera, which I also immediately handed over.

The two men left and ran away into the bushes. Fausto was upset. He complained that I gave away my things too quickly. When I reminded him of the shovel attack, he seemed to agree with me that it probably had been wise not to resist. Fausto felt betrayed by the men, because, on other occasions, Mario had asked Fausto to help him to rob someone else, so Fausto felt that he was one of them, not classified as fair game to be robbed.

I guess my presence was far too tempting for Mario to resist, and that this overpowered the feeling of camaraderie he had with Fausto. Also I was a stranger, an outsider, someone they had never seen before and would probably never see again. Fausto felt guilty and stupid for having led me into such a dangerous situation: Osvaldo had been right in running away as soon as he could. The situation was certainly risky, but I had trusted Fausto's judgment and familiarity with the people and the environment. I had overlooked the fact that Fausto was drunk and his judgment impaired.

After a few minutes, the gang of young men who had gone to the bushes to have the orgy returned to the road to see why we were taking so long to go down to the river. We told them what had happened and they seemed surprised and a bit disgusted by the turn of events. Rivereño looked especially upset. After a few minutes of discussion they went back to the bushes in pursuit of the two robbers. I was never sure if this was a plot, specifically a sting so a few could rob me and later the rest could share the marijuana bought with the stolen money. I especially thought this when Fausto told me later that Rivereño was also a robber. I wondered if these others would have robbed me had I gotten to the river with my possessions.

I also wondered whether Fausto and I being obvious homosexuals was the stimulus for the robbers. That is, it is well known that sissies do not defend themselves. I was also wearing open, thong-like sandals, which made me quite vulnerable. I could not easily run away or pursue the robbers, nor could I give a painful, swift quick in the groin to my attacker. Fausto pointed this out after the robbery. He said that they saw me as being so harmless and defenseless walking without sensible shoes.

That was not the only time I inadvertently advertised the helplessness that marks a male for domination and worse. I was not trying to attract the attention of *hombres*, but as in the incident just related, I sometimes unconsciously incited *hombres* in ways that even so flamboyant a *loca* as Osvaldo thought reckless.

When walking with Osvaldo, I noticed that most of the time men would yell catcalls at Osvaldo and never at me, even though I was hanging out with him. On a superficial level, one may imagine that if what Osvaldo wants is to sexually attract *hombres*, then his looks are appropriate since he is getting *hombres'* attention (although as I showed in the previous chapters, many *hombres* actually prefer to date homosexuals who are not too visible or obvious). On the street many *hombres* tease *locas* and by doing so they seem to show their desire toward the obvious homosexuals.

One time, however, I was walking with Osvaldo when an *hombre* with erotically-charged language approached me first, rather than Osvaldo. It was the first time that it ever happened and, as I learned later, it was because I was adopting a stance culturally marked as feminine. I made a feminine gesture, though only for a few seconds, this was enough to attract an *hombre* (and I am sure that being beside of Osvaldo already attracted attention).

The situation was as follows: On a Thursday in September of 1997, Osvaldo and I were walking in downtown San Pedro. It was at dusk: 6:45 PM. A *cipote* (teenager) who was selling something approached me on my right side (Osvaldo was on my left) and said to me "Mi amor" ("my love"), which could be considered a *piropo*. Then he said "*¿Cómo estás?*" ("how are you?") and I said *"Bien"* ("good"). Then Osvaldo told me not to talk to him. The *cipote* continued with "*¿Me vas a dar algo?*" ("Are you going to give me something?"). I did not reply. Next the *cipote* walked behind us and went to Osvaldo's side and said aimed some *piropos* at him. Osvaldo did not reply, and eventually the youth said "Adiós" ("bye") and left.

Osvaldo said that the *cipote* was a *"choz"* or *"chocero"* (robber, from *"chocear,"* to steal). Osvaldo said the *cipote* grabbed Osvaldo's ass before leaving. He also said that the *cipote* was accompanied by two other persons. According to Osvaldo, these people had asked the *cipote* if he was going to continue pursuing us, or was going to join them. He joined them while Osvaldo and I kept walking. I was surprised because this was the very first time in my stay in Honduras that an *hombre* had teased me. I asked Osvaldo why this time **I** was the one who had been teased. Osvaldo had no doubt that the reason why I was identified as a homosexual this time was that I was holding the water bottles I had just bought against my chest with crisscrossed arms—which is a feminine manner, according to Osvaldo, who is conscious of the ways in which gender is read (whether or not it is intentionally written). An *hombre* would have carried the bottles hanging down or on his shoulder, but never clutch them against his chest with crossed arms.

Although I escaped being gang-raped, the *hombres* took their toll. Another way in which *hombres* demonstrate their territoriality is by teasing a *loca* when he passes by, in a way not much different from the *piropo*[2] aimed at women. *Piropos* are another kind of charge for passing through *hombre* territory (which is close to being any public space).

Desire + Contempt = Teasing ?

Joking relationships have long been studied in anthropology. Depending on the culture and historical period, joking relationships have been found to be limited to some types of relationships, while avoidance is normative for others. Perhaps because joking—and sexual teasing—deal with desire and anger simultaneously, a very fine line divides joke from insult. If a cultural boundary is trespassed, joking can suddenly become an insult rather than a ritualized game.[3]

---

2. A *piropo* is a flirtatiously embellished remark, usually cried out loudly in the public from a man to a woman, but sometimes from an *hombre* to a *loca*.

Peter Lyman explains sexist jokes and other types of joking that take place among males as a way of maintaining male group bonding. All-male joking, which might be perceived as offensive or vulgar by some-one who does not belong to the group, is nevertheless considered "funny" and as proof of "coolness" among their peers. As Lyman put it:

> Jokes indirectly express the emotions and tensions that may disrupt everyday life by "negotiating" them, reconstituting group solidarity by shared aggression and cathartic laughter. The ordinary conse-quences of forbidden words are suspended by meta-linguistic ges-tures (tones of voice, facial expressions, catch phrases) that send the message "this is a joke," and emotions that would ordinarily endan-ger a social relationship can be spoken safely within the micro-world created by the "joke form." (1995:87)

According to David L. Collinson (1995[1988]:164) "The ability to produce a laugh is a defining characteristic of group membership." If one of the parties does not want to collaborate, then it is not a joke anymore. Joking needs cooperation. If joking is used opportunely, tense situations that might have otherwise escalated to higher forms of conflict are defused. Through joking, things that would have otherwise been impossible to mention, suddenly can be said. People do not only relax but also "let off steam" by laughing. The fact that they are laugh-ing together is a reflection that they are willing to "work"—at least in the joking realm—as a team.

Much like male or co-worker bonding, sexual teasing expressed in the form of the *piropo* in Latin America, most of the time from a man to a woman, but sometimes from an *hombre* to a *loca*, can be used to dissolve interpersonal tension and open up new avenues of communi-cation—communication that might go from verbal to physical, having a sexual contact with the teased being its ultimate goal. Sexual/erotic desire, then, is often first expressed through teasing.

---

3.   Insults can also be ritualized, with a thin line between "playful" bandiage and serious insults. See Murray 1979.

Sexual teasing in the form of flirtatious comments and provocative body language is normative behavior within the courting protocol of Latin American *hombres*. The fact that teasing is not only directed toward females but also toward other males in the "culture of machismo" is, perhaps, less known.

According to Brandes (1981:223), in everyday Latino conversation, claims to phallic supremacy over women coincide with "a constant attempt to force masculine rivals into the feminine role, in a never-ending quest to avoid adopting the role themselves."[4] Latino men talking obsessively about "tomarlo por culo" do not expect those they tell "¡Baja los pantalones!" actually to drop their pants and take it up the ass right there and then, any more than they expect the women they leer at and sling *piropos* at are going to stop and give themselves to their "suitors." Both kinds of talk are ritualistic. To label them "ritualistic" doesn't mean that the behavior lacks motivation. Indeed, it doesn't take much depth psychology to suspect insecurity about masculinity in those who incessantly parade their interest in sexual conquests. ("Real men" do it and don't have to brag about it.)

Remarks about women's desirability may express aesthetic appreciation, some *hombres* claim. The sexual explicitness of most instances makes it hard to believe that much sublimation occurs in such behavior, however.[5] Gardner (1980, 1995) suggested that men are desensitized to sexual rejection by such (very unequal) "exchanges," while women learn to ignore male importuning. Carrier (1995) noted that

---

4.   Brandes was writing about Andalusia. Lumsden (1991:22) makes a similar claim about México, and Reinhardt (in Murray 1995:152) about Chicanos in the United States.

5.   Along with contending that the real audience for *piropos* is male bystanders ("the aim is to make other men laugh or be impressed"), Prieur (1998:219) noted that some *piropos* are flattering and appreciative rather than coarse and humiliating. She sees *piropos* of both source "as a demonstration of men's power to categorize women, to label them as attractive or unattractive. I regard it as a ritual affirmation of masculinity."

the guys who were really interested in having sex with me and
Alberto [both publicly known to be sexually available] would also
enter into the joking and be quite crude, but when they wanted to
negotiate a sexual encounter it would be done discreetly, out of ear-
shot from the others. They never wanted any of their friends to
know for sure that sex had taken place, so some non-sexual pretext
was always made for going off alone with either of us.

By camouflaging desire through teasing, casual auditors/observers
are never sure if what the *hombre* is saying is true or not. By saying
what he says in an outrageous way, the *hombre* sweeps away from his
displays of desire any trace of seriousness, guarding his otherwise objec-
tionable behavior from societal condemnation. Moreover, teasing is
used as a way to let the other party know that he is willing and ready
for sexual activity without risking outright rejection ("I was only joking
around").

Teasing is a relatively safe way to begin a sexual transaction with the
other. "Would you be available to have sex with me?" the teaser seems
to be asking. By responding as part of the joke, by enabling the joke to
survive, by collaborating in it, the person teased seems to be saying, "I
might consider it."

Yet many times a *loca* has no choice but to collaborate with the joke.
Otherwise he might be attacked by the *hombre*. Therefore, the equation tease = desire in the relationship *hombre/loca* is not complete, as
contempt (expressed in violence against *locas*) seems to be an important
part of it as well. The same *hombres* who tease *locas* may be the ones
who mistreat them, full of contempt, if *locas* do not respond appropriately to their jokes. In the Honduran lower-class, where *hombre/loca*
teasing occurs to the greatest extent, violence against *locas* is commonplace. The following incident shows how easily the line from teasing to
violence is crossed.

While joking relationships between *hombres* and *locas* alleviate tensions created by the socially condemned homoerotic attraction that
exist between them—expressed in the need to attract each other's

attention—the equation is delicately balanced and can easily lead to violence. If the *loca* decides not to collaborate in the joke, usually by ignoring it, the *hombre* may feel insulted. The *loca* may also feel insulted if he takes the *piropo*, joke or teasing as a demonstration of disrespect rather than a tribute to his desirability. The fact that many times the *loca* decides to collaborate with the joke for fear of physical retaliation on the part of the *hombres* shows the socially disadvantageous position that the *loca* occupies in Honduran society.

Lack of deference to the *hombre* in any realm, not just joking, may lead to violence against the *loca*. This, along with the example of toll-charging and violence due to *hombre* territoriality, reveals hierarchies of gender and sexuality that disfavor the *loca*.

8

HIDING AND FLAUNTING HOMOSEXUALITY

The claim that sexuality in Latin America is something that cannot be brought out in the public is only partially true. While I agree with the assertion that only recently—primarily because of the AIDS epidemic—sexuality has been perforce put in the public discourse to the embarrassment of pious and puritanical eyes and ears, I must add here that the primary difference between now and then has been that now the talk about sexuality is being done in a serious way.

For a long time in Latin America sexuality has been brought up in public discourse. But this has mostly been done in a joking fashion rather than as part of serious discussion or debate. The way that sexuality was publicly dealt with in the past was in the form of *picardía*—jokes, double entendres in songs and mass media and in joking relationships between people.[1]

La picardía

To talk with *picardía* means to make what one says less blunt, bold or direct. *Picardía* is an indirect and humorous way to refer to sex as it uses double entendre and funny metaphors in its narrative. In *picardía* knowledge is nuanced and made more subtle by "spicing" or "season-

---

1.   I owe this insight to three gay Latina/os at present living in the US: the Chilean Andrés Sciolla, the Puerto Rican Manolo Flores, and the Mexican-American Grace Rosales.

ing" it with mischievous humor: *picardía* is like hot sauce, *una salsa que pica*, or itches in the mouth. *Picardía* itches in a savory way, when the listener enters into complicity with the speaker, for this esoteric news has been disclosed in double entendre that only initiates (*entendidos*) can fully share.

Picardía is commonly found in popular songs and in broadcasters' speech—a safe way to talk about sex in public. For example, a popular *cómputo* song in Honduras during the fall of 1998 had as its main lyric the words "jalando cometas" [pulling the kite], which makes an allusion to penile masturbation, because of the similarity in the hand movement between pulling a kite and pulling the prepuce. Using *picardía* to describe masturbation makes the song funny and appealing for the people who could capture the metaphor; explicitly naming masturbation in the song in an open way would have been considered to be in extremely poor taste.

Yet this situation has, in recent years, been changing in Latin America as it is becoming more and more common to see serious, direct, and controversial debates in respectable mass media on sexuality and reproductive rights, including matters of premarital sex, teen pregnancy, abortion, contraception, and homosexuality. A clear example of this is Peruvian-born Jaime Bayly's work. His 1994 book, appropriately titled *No se lo digas a nadie* (*Don't tell it to anyone*), openly deals with homosexuality and has become a best seller in the Spanish speaking world. Bayly also conducts the interview show "En directo" that is broadcast to the Americas on CBS-TV cable. In his interviews, Bayly deals with the topic of sexuality in a rather direct way by Latin American public standards (although far less openly than many television talk-show hosts in the US).

"Drama"

Along with covert ways of speaking about homosexual attractions and acts in ways that hostile nonparticipants will miss, there is an intra-*ambiente* art of embellishment, which Honduran *locas* call "drama."

The "art" consists of exaggerating or simply lying when describing within the *ambiente* sexual encounters, conquests, etc. My interpretation of this phenomenon is that it is done as an entertaining form of socializing, but also, on occasion, to elicit information. Most importantly, through drama, *locas* construct the ideal *hombre*, thereby keeping alive the fantasy which is one of the pillars of their sexual culture.

Why do *locas* use the term "drama"? "Lying" has a negative connotation. "Drama," on the other hand, is a playful: a theatrical way to convey a message. It requires some acting skills, otherwise the lie will be discovered. Drama can be outrageous, as in camp, or serious, as in envious competition. In any case, there is always something funny about such drama: stories are just too good (or too bad) to be real.

Lying to elicit information

On Friday, October 3, 1997, I went on an excursion to a river close to San Pedro along with Osvaldo, Fausto, and Freddie. Of the group, only Freddie considered himself heterosexual or *hombre*. Rivers close to San Pedro are usually surrounded by dense tropical rainforest and few people go there, giving the necessary privacy for a sexual encounter that is not possible at home because of overcrowded conditions (see Murray 1987: 123-24; 1995: 38-43). As we approached the river, an unspoken tension grew that something "sexual" might occur. Rivers are also known to be dangerous spots because the same isolation that makes them ideal places for sexual encounters also makes them ideal places for robbers. Thus, our tacit tension was not only caused by sexual anticipations but also by well-founded fears of attack.

Once on the riverbank, Freddie started sexually harassing Osvaldo by trying to pinch Osvaldo's buttocks and insisting that Osvaldo should give oral sex to him. Osvaldo resisted and Freddie, semi-annoyed, semi-playful, chased Osvaldo away, down the riverbank, by throwing little stones at Osvaldo. Unfortunately, one of the stones hit Osvaldo on the hand, opening a small but painful bleeding wound on it. Osvaldo was very upset and remained down the river by himself. Fausto, Freddie, and I stayed up-river, in the bushes.

The next day, Osvaldo told me that Helvecio (another gender non-conforming, homosexually identified man who knew all of us who had gone to the river the day before) claimed to know "everything" that had happened at the river the day before. Among all the things Osvaldo said Helvecio claimed had happened was that I fellated Freddie while we were in the bushes. I told Osvaldo that this did not happen. Osvaldo insisted that someone told Helvecio that *I* gave oral sex to Freddie. Who could have told such a lie to Helvecio? Only Fausto, Freddie, and I were in the bushes at that time. Did Fausto or Freddie tell this lie to Helvecio?

Since Osvaldo was not present when I was with Freddie in the bushes, Osvaldo was not sure whether I gave oral sex to Freddie or not. Although the night before I did tell Osvaldo that "nothing" had happened when we were in the bushes, Osvaldo might have thought that perhaps I was not telling him the truth. Later, Osvaldo told me that many times *locas* get truth out of a lie. By lying they get truthful information. I then realized that Osvaldo was doing that with me earlier on. Nobody told Helvecio that I had fellated Freddie. Osvaldo invented that part of the story to see my reaction. Had I reacted with shock, like I was caught out, Osvaldo would have known that the night before I lied to him and that I really did give oral sex to Freddie. But because I firmly denied that that was true, and showed myself rather skeptical of the whole story, Osvaldo confirmed that I really did not give oral sex to Freddie. Had I been an accomplished liar, however, I would have anticipated Osvaldo's lies to elicit some truth from me and I would have reacted exactly the way I reacted, regardless if it were true or not. I would have always denied it, shown myself skeptical about the issue, and made up some drama about it; or perhaps I would have "confirmed" Osvaldo's suspicions by lying about how fantastic the oral sex that I gave to Freddie was in order to make Osvaldo jealous. When I realized this, I confronted Osvaldo, who confessed he had wanted to

double check whether I had told him the truth about not having fellated Freddie at the river the day before.

Lying as camp

It is interesting to witness a conversation between Helvecio and
Osvaldo, two accomplished performers in the art of lying. With them,
nobody is certain what is truth and what is drama. It is the art of performing a reality whatever this is. It is campy.[2] It seems that both parties, in this case Osvaldo and Helvecio, are enjoying the game
enormously. The stories get more and more outrageous as both parties
prove their mastery in the art of drama. Someone not trained or
unaware of the game will "fall" as soon as he or she tells the truth. I can
imagine that it is more fun to keep on with the drama, although at
some point the need to know some truth may appear. Each time
Osvaldo talks to someone who is a master of drama, I later ask him
what was truth and what was drama. Osvaldo is never completely positive about what was true. He is left in doubt. For revenge, the next
time he talks to the person, Osvaldo will tell him fantastic stories to
make him jealous.

Envy and competition

Part of drama is based on envy and competition, always focusing on
the handsomest men and the largest penis. As for gay ritual insults in
the US, success requires keeping one's cool while exceeding in outra-
geousness what the other player produces to disparage one (see Murray
1979). In drama the listener will dismiss the story by telling another
one that is even more fantastic, hyperbolic, and outrageous. Both par-

---

2.   Núñez Noriega (1994) sees camp as part of an identity as it reflects a sense of
      difference (from the heterosexual and heterosexist world) and similarity (within
      homosexual social networks): "Camp is a synthesis of gazes: an external and an
      internal one; and the product of this double vision characterizes the sensitivity
      of a gay man" (p. 310). On the general notion of "camp[ing]" see White 1998.

ties draw pleasure from this drama contest. It does not matter what is true and what is not. What matters is who creates the most outrageous story. Drama becomes pure entertainment. Does this emerge from a necessity to connect with the other while coping with feelings of envy? Is it a harmless way to tease each other while spending time together? Prieur reported observing competitive bragging among *locas* or *jotas*:

> In the span of a couple of hours I witnessed the following confrontations: first Pancha and Angela competed about who had the nicest home. Pancha won, since her home was bigger, less crowded, and materially better equipped. But Angela took her revenge, by stating that she could walk about as she pleased at home, wearing miniskirt and makeup and be treated like a woman. Pancha knew this was a weak point, but said she wore her foam-rubber paddings at home. This was an obvious loss and everybody laughed. (1998:169)

Locas like to boast about their conquests. This has also been reported as occurring in the Philippines where Hart (1992:215-16) saw this as "an excellent validation of his sex-role inversion." Instead of resorting to negative psychological explanations one may, instead, see the boasting drama as friendly competition, which strengthens social bonding while helping players cope with feelings of envy or inferiority. Lying as campy boasting might be related to the commonly seen desire of *locas* to be seen as upper-class, beautiful, and distinguished—what in Chile is called "regia." This has also to do with the "theatrical" tendencies of the *loca* (female impersonation) and love for beauty pageants, both of which can be seen as rituals of inversion, or, according to Kulick (1998), as rituals of intensification, because *locas* personify and crystallize in themselves societal conceptions of gender and sexuality.

Competition in drama, however, many times goes beyond drama itself and reflects competition for something specific; for instance, who first seduces an attractive *hombre*. In this case, drama is used as an effective tool to deceive other contestants and win the game:

MIGUEL: For example, if there is an *hombre* who [I find] hand-some, [but whom] you [also] like, to make you lose interest in him I will tell you, "he's *avicuti!*," so you don't go with him. Or "this [other] one is *cafú!*," to fool you, so you get involved with him only to find out that he's *avicuti.*"
MANUEL: Why would someone like to do that?
MIGUEL: To be mischievous.

Identifying drama

I asked Osvaldo how he could tell when Helvecio is making up drama and when he is not. Osvaldo told me that he could tell because of the sarcastic tone of the conversation. Drama is often sarcastic. There is another difference that I noticed and that Osvaldo confirmed: drama speech is slower and more pronounced; each word is carefully high-lighted, unlike in regular speech. Yet the differences are too subtle to be detected by the untrained ear. If one is not familiar with it, one will surely not tune into the "drama frequency" or will tune into it too late, invariably making oneself the fool by revealing information that other-wise one would not have wanted made public and by believing as true what everyone else trained in the art recognizes as "drama."

Causing *un escándalo*

"Oppression in the form of 'invisibilization' comes through a refusal of legitimate public existence…. Virtual denial of their existence often forces them [the feminized] to resort to the weapons of the weak, which confirm the stereotypes." (Bourdieu 2001:119, 59)

The final kind of speech event I want to discuss involves homosex-ual males calling attention to themselves (the opposite of *picardía* in courting danger) in public. A somewhat comedic self-dramatization, unlike "drama," which is enacted for fellow homosexuals within the *ambiente*, the audience for "scandalizing" is *hombres* in their aspect as potential sexual partners rather than as fagbashers (*matacabros*, literally sheep-killers).

On Sunday in October of 1998, Osvaldo and I went to the beach of Omoa, close to Puerto Cortés. Osvaldo was wearing tight jeans hiked up to his thighs. This garb showed off the full length of his shaved legs, and his swishy walk accentuated the rounded, full buttocks tightly packed in the jeans. The way he dressed immediately attracted the attention of men (and women). At the beach Osvaldo stripped off his mini-shorts off to a tiny woman's bikini or *tanga*. He was also wearing a long, white shirt that covered the *tanga*, so that it looked as if he was wearing a miniskirt dress. In the water the shirt turned transparent, so the black *tanga* could be seen through the shirt. We walked along the beach. In an area with many young men in the water, Osvaldo caused a commotion. Men yelled *piropos*, whistled, etc. We kept walking and Osvaldo totally ignored them. Suddenly, a piece of ice fell close to us. Next, a rain of chunks of ice (quite big, like rocks) fell in front of us. They had been thrown from behind us, so they had flown over our heads, very close to us before falling just in front of us. Any of these big pieces of ice (each the size of a polo ball) could have hit us, hurting us badly. Luckily, none did. Enraged, I turned toward the men who had yelled the *piropos*. They calmed down immediately, affected by my visibly angry reaction. However, I could not figure out which of them had thrown the ice.

Later I asked Osvaldo why he dresses so flamboyantly. I asked him if he liked to cause a commotion, paraphrasing Kulick's idea (1996) that transgendered people can self-empower themselves and exert agency by causing a commotion or public scandal.[3] Osvaldo replied, yes, that he

---

3.   The scandals or commotions that Kulick describes for Brazilian transgendered prostitutes, however, are very different of a kind, consisting mainly of the transvestites calling their *hombre* clients "*maricona*" in front of other people, which suggests that the *hombre* client has been penetrated by the transvestite—a shocking reversal of "the natural order" of masculine-looking men penetrating.

likes to be noticed and to receive acknowledgment of his desirability. More importantly, he said, he dresses in such a way because he feels more comfortable. I asked him how he could feel more comfortable with clothes which are so tight. He replied that he has always been used to wearing tight clothes. When he wears loose clothes, Osvaldo said he feels uncomfortable, heavy, etc. Then I asked him how can he feel more comfortable when he provokes the aggression of people, such as when the ice was thrown at us. He claimed that the reason they threw the ice at us was solely based on his non-response to their *piropos*, and not to the scandal he caused by his appearance *per se*. In other words, if he dresses like that, he will excite men. Once they are excited, if he ignores them, the men will become angry and attack. But if he teases them back, the situation would not escalate beyond verbal jokes. Osvaldo many times claimed that *hombres* will only physically attack him (or his friends) if he or his friends ignore *hombres* after having excited them.

I inquired more formally about the issue during my last interview with him in October 1998:

> INTERVIEWER: Why do you look so *obvio*? Would it be possible that if you wanted to you could look less *obvio*?
> OSVALDO: Well, I don't think it's possible, since I've tried it on several occasions with no success. I've made the effort to even imitate ways of walking that are different from what I'm used to. Once a friend and I practiced, which we called "stepping on ants." It consists of making the gesture of killing ants with the feet as one steps, but not even this worked out. So I've tried several times. Even walking like a robot, that is, mechanically—all *cuadrado*—but nothing, nothing has worked. I believe that it's something natural which each one of us brings with oneself. For some people, walking with mannerisms is part of us. It's not an attitude that one may want to take, because no one likes to be humiliated or harassed by other people.
> I: But your being *obvio* isn't only a way of walking. It's also the

way you do your eyebrows, your hair, the clothes you wear, your high-heeled shoes: those things could be avoided. If you don't use those things you'd look much less *obvio*, wouldn't you?

O: Yes, but I wouldn't feel well. I have some loose clothes that you can say are for *cuadrados*; these clothes are even a few numbers larger than my size. But in that moment, when I wear those clothes, I don't feel right. It feels like it isn't me. I don't identify with it. And at the same time I don't feel well, because when I look at the mirror I look ugly. Say, aesthetically, to my standards, those clothes don't look good on me.

I: So even if people yell things at you on the street because you look *obvio*, that is less negative than the feeling you get from dressing as a "heterosexual"?

O: Yes, exactly. It's less negative because that I can somehow tolerate it, while the internal part is a conflict that I almost don't control; twenty years had to pass before I could solve my own identity or sexual orientation and accept my personality. To try to change internally, not to feel uncomfortable in certain clothes, would take me a long time. It's not that I can't do it. Perhaps it's possible. But it's difficult.

I: It's easier to tolerate people yelling at you on the streets?

O: Yes.

...

I: How could a homosexual at whom people are yelling things on the street or in a public place, avoid violence?

O: If one doesn't want to have any more trouble or is in a quiet mood and wants to have a good day, what one does is, when they say "*adiós*" ["good-bye"], one answers back in a nice way, just like they did it. Or if they say "*hola*" ["hello'] and they tell you "*Mi amor, ¿qué tal está?*" ["My love, how are you?"], one replies "*Bien, cariño* ["I'm fine, darling"], *adiós*, bye-bye".

I: And in that way they don't react with violence?

O: No, they don't react with violence because somehow they feel like—reinforced in their self-esteem. [They feel] they were heard. Even if they don't admit this: [un]consciously they want to feel the answer of the homosexual, that the homosexual has paid attention to them.

I: I would like to ask you something else: when you go out *colorinche* [flashy] to the streets and create a scandal, is it a situation that you weren't looking for, does it inevitably happen because you were carrying yourself in a *colorinche* way, or were you also intending to create a scandal?

O: Well, sometimes. Other times it depends on the occasion. Sometimes we people are in a low mood. Then we need to feel that we exist, feel that we are visible in this world. So we wear certain clothes, certain shoes that call people's attention, and we hit the streets so that people will be scandalized. We go out *colorinches*. And other times we don't.

I: So it's not only that you just are the way you are and you can't change because if you do you'd suffer, you'd feel you aren't yourself anymore and the reaction of people on the street is something you simply can't avoid. You also are actually looking for that reaction on the street; you actively want to have that reaction from people. And if nothing happens, how would you feel?

O: Well, it wouldn't affect me much either. It depends on my mood, but most times it doesn't affect me at all.

I: Most times when you've caused a scandal, does it give you pleasure, do you like it, or would you rather [wish] that wouldn't have happened, or perhaps do you have a combination of both feelings?

O: Sometimes I enjoy it. Sometimes I don't. And sometimes it's a combination of both feelings. Sometimes I feel angry because I'd like to remain invisible and not be the center of attraction in that moment. But I have to accept it at times, that, well, **most times**, I catch people's attention.

I: Besides the times when you enjoy it because that was really what you were looking for, are there times that you enjoy it because the type of scandal people are doing for you is a type of scandal that you like? Are there times when you don't enjoy the scandal because you don't like that type of scandal? Does it only depend on your mood whether you enjoy a scandal or not?

O: No, it also depends on that [on the type of scandal].

I: What's the difference between both types of scandal?

O: One of them feels offensive at times. People try to stigmatize you as an easy person, like a whore. Sometimes people see me on the streets and yell "whore", "prostitute" or any other word alike (laughter).

I: And do you like that or not?

O: No, I don't like it, because I'm really not a whore. If I were one, I wouldn't feel offended, because [prostitution] is a job like any other; someone has to do it.

I: So what's the kind of scandal you enjoy? What do people say to you?

O: Well (laughter), the scandal I like is educated, sensual, exotic; it uses words that please the ear.

I: Like a *piropo* rather than an insult?

O: That's it. Exactly.

I: Do you remember any? [Pause.] Or your favorite [*piropo*]; the one you like most.

O: Well, I like it when they say "*mamacita*" ["Mommie"] (laughter). Or "*linda*" ["pretty female"], "*belleza*" ["beauty"], "*amorcita*" ["lovely female"]. Words like that make one feel complimented when listening to them.

I: Like affectionate words.

O: Uh-huh. Exactly!

I: But the tone in which they say it, is it affectionate?

O: Yes, affectionate.

I: Isn't it ironic?

O: No. Well, sometimes it is. But most times it's affectionate. They say it because they really mean it, though they define themselves as heterosexuals.

I: Would you say that there is some sexual charge, desire, in the tone?

O: Yes, I think so. Most times yes, that's it. Even though they don't consider themselves anything but simply heterosexuals.

I: And would you say that the tone resembles the tone of the *piropos* directed to an attractive woman? Is there a difference?

O: No, I think they are similar, the same tone. I don't see any difference.

I: Would you then say that the pleasure that those *piropos* directed to you provoke in you has to do with the fact that these *piropos* make you feel like an attractive woman?

O: No, I don't think so. Before I used to be like that, [cherishing] that idea of feeling almost like an attractive woman. But not anymore. I've accepted my masculinity and I feel very good about the way I am.

I: This question about if you really liked some kinds of scandal comes from something you told me last year. You said that when you [and a group of other *locas*] went to El Salvador nobody yelled anything at you on the streets and you began to feel insecure; like "What's going on, is there something wrong about us here?" But as soon as you crossed the border back to Honduras people again were yelling *piropos* at you. With a sigh of relief you said: "Thank God, people are making a scandal for us again!"—almost as if you really needed it.

O: Yes, say, as I told you, sometimes one needs to feel that one is visible, that one exists; that people look at one for x or y reason. And there are times when one doesn't—

I: Does it have to do with that you may like a scandal depending on the context? Say, it isn't the same being called "mamacita" walking on 15th street and 14th avenue than being called "mamacita" in front of your house or being called "mamacita" in your workplace.

O: Yes, it also depends on the context. As you say, the site has lots to do with it, because sometimes, for example in the workplace, I don't like people crying *piropos* at me because what I'm doing there is a job, I'm getting paid for working, not for receiving *piropos* or being seduced by anyone…. Say, in the mechanics [of causing a scandal], there are several situations, subjects, contexts and elements involved. I'd say the main subjects involved are the homosexual and the person making the scandal, or the subject who is seducing [the homosexual] and the context would be the place, the moment: the workplace, the street, a recreation place. And the time, the moment. However, it all depends on the context and one's mood. Sometimes one really doesn't want to create a scandal but it happens anyway.

Especially when cruising for sexual partners, effeminate homosexuals "very consciously treat their bodes as carriers of signs…sent to possible sexual partners. The first part of the message is: "I'm sexually available, come and get it!' The second part is: 'You may forget I'm a man; you don't have to worry: I'll be like a woman for you," as Prieur (1998:222) translated such self-presentation.

9

THE "AMERICAN WAY"?

The promise of the commodification of sexuality (as a part of globalization) was to free gender and sexuality from traditional strictures by offering, through commercial fashions, ever-changing models of bodily presentation. However, as sexuality has become "liberalized" and commodified, a widening schism in homosexual cultures has appeared. Similarly to the increasing socioeconomic inequality fostered by economic neoliberalism, the neoliberalization of sexual politics in Latin America has also widened the gap of inequality among participants of local homosexual cultures, as one very specific model of gayness have been privileged over others.

During the late-1970s, the term *gay* started to be used in some major urban centers, and rapidly spread to the rest of urban Latin America during the early-1980s (Murray and Arboleda, 1987 1995). *Gay* came to signify an imagined gay identity existing in "the North" (the USA, Canada, northwestern Europe) for which there must also be local embodiments of homosexual conduct and desires. The "American" way of being gay was largely a construct made of imagined and romanticized images of gay freedom and happiness in an equally imagined paradise of general affluence.[1]

This new "gay lifestyle" was initially appropriated by an economic elite, which had the means to travel and to imitate trends in the gay ghettoes of New York, Los Angeles, or San Francisco.[2] The "American Way"—a culture of consumerism, sexual freedom, and privacy, with relatively costly gay venues and the possibility to live alone or with a partner, away from familial surveillance—could be emulated by only a very few. For the same reason, several early Latin American homosexual political organizations rejected the term, because it represented foreign values, US imperialism, and elitism (Murray and Arboleda 1995:142).[3] During the late 1980s and early 1990s, however, the term *gay* became mainstream within the homosexual cultures of Latin America and lost, to a certain extent, its connotations of privilege and status. The "gay lifestyle" was astutely marketed by ambitious entrepreneurs, who promoted gay-oriented businesses (including bars with named for places the USA or northwestern Europe) .

The popularization of the term *gay* and of new gay identities was also a consequence of the AIDS epidemic, which since the mid-1980s affected the male homosexual population of the major urban centers of Latin America (NACLA Report on the Americas 1998; Altman 1996). AIDS forced the discourses about sexuality to become more public than ever before (see Adam, Duyvendak, and Krouwel, 1999; Carrillo 2002). This created much tension, as sexuality had traditionally belonged to the realm of the unspeakable. Speaking about sexual transmission thrust forward the figure of the homosexual as a serious topic of public discussion for the first time in Latin American history. Emerging homosexual organizations, which, during the 1970s and

1. *Gay* did not signify a homogenous and uniform identity in the US. As the literature on gay identities and movements in the United States (see Adam 1987, Murray 1996a) and the queer theory critique of identity politics (see Sedgwick 1990, Butler 1990) effectively demonstrate, the multiplicity of identities surrounding same-sex desire, homoerotic aesthetics, and homosexual subcultures cannot be reduced to a single and monolithic "gay identity" or "gay culture." There is similar danger of essentializing the "American Way" or simply "America" (see Pettett 1999).

2. This is not the case for every Latin American country. In certain urban cultures of Brazil, for example, the term *gay* was initially appropriated by gender nonconforming *travestis* of low SES who claimed it for themselves as an identity (see Green 1999).

3. As Altman (1996, 1997) pointed out, the very discourses against the globalizing effects of the "American" gay model were also globalized appropriations of "First World" subaltern-theory narratives.

1980s had barely managed to survive and remained largely ignored, suddenly became more visible and viable.

Organizations for the rights of homosexuals that had lacked funds and members began receiving financial assistance from international organizations. Many of these local gay groups were reorganized into NGOs under the aegis of being AIDS organizations during the 1990s. Thanks to AIDS-related funding, the homosexual movement in Latin America was able to flourish as never before during the 1990s (see Fernández-Alemany and Larson 1996, Fernández-Alemany 1999). Throughout Latin America, however, while an imagined "American" gay identity has been tacitly or indirectly promoted in AIDS organizations and politics, HSH, the Spanish equivalent of MSM, or men who have sex with men, has been preferred by these AIDS groups to escape identity binding and focus on sexual behavior.

In Honduras, however, *gay* has not entered the language of colloquial conversation. *Homosexual* is the term most commonly used. *Gay* is only used in Honduras in two very specific contexts: social networks of elite persons and organizations working for the human rights of sexual minorities and people living with HIV/AIDS.

The politics of gender and the politics of sexuality

Differences between the politics of sexuality and the politics of gender have often been overlooked in Latin American sexual politics. Along with classism and sexism, the influx of AIDS-prevention money during the 1990s, and the commodification of sexuality have further marginalized nonelite women and transgendered persons. During the 1970s and 1980s, some women and men worked together in the early and weak homosexual rights groups in Latin America (although other lesbians chose to work within women's organizations). But as these groups became stronger with the inflow of money for AIDS prevention and education, lesbians felt excluded. Fighting against patriarchal structures of domination and sexism were not given priority, despite the fact that the fight against what was perceived as being heterosexual male hegemony was also in the best interest of homosexual men (see Klein 1998:32).

Transgendered persons, especially transvestites, also felt marginalized by mainstream "AIDS Inc." The new AIDS campaigns depicted a North American ideal of male homosexuality with iconic middle-class, consumerist. masculine-looking gay males. Transvestites who, throughout Latin America, subsist in the lower socioeconomic statuses and cannot afford the idealized North American model of gay lifestyle, felt excluded. Moreover, their gender-variant bodily presentation was not included in the new imagery and narrative about masculine gay clones imported from the First World and promoted by AIDS Inc.. In Honduras, transvestites felt alienated from the new AIDS/gay organizations, which they felt either ignored or further denigrated them. For instance, AIDS groups claimed that cleaning the city of transgendered prostitutes would help to control the epidemic. As a reaction to this, some transgendered people reaffirmed their autonomy and rejected this rhetoric and continue earning their living as street prostitutes (see Kulick 1998 for an analysis of a similar situation in Brazil). Prostitution really is the only type of work that transgendered people are allowed to do in Honduras. Transgender people's decision to protect their right to practice prostitution then does not only come from a pure liberal motivation based on full agency and free choice, but is also the reaction to societal structures of oppression that constrain them to the very restricted and marginalized space of prostitution as the only way to earn their money.

Homophobic landscapes

AIDS also produced a homophobic backlash in the form of hate crimes and the closure of most of the new gay locales in countries such as Honduras. Studying newspaper reports on violence against homosexual and gender nonconforming people in Honduras, Richard Elliott reached the conclusion that there was a connection between the appearance of the first AIDS cases after 1985 and the dramatic rise of hate crimes. At least in the beginnings of the epidemic, people blamed homosexuals for being AIDS vectors (Elliott 1995, 1996a, 1996b:22).

The homophobia raised by the AIDS epidemic also might have had to do with a new visibility of homosexuals that threatened to subvert the heterosexist and patriarchal order of things. As such, this "new" violence was the reflection of an old and deeply ingrained homophobia (see Elliott 1996:40-1, Inforpress Centroamericana 1994:4). This seems to be supported by what 72-year-old Don Pedro told me in 1994:

> INTERVIEWER: And as time was passing, what changes did you see in San Pedro's homosexual *ambiente*?
> DON PEDRO: No, I retired [quit the *ambiente*] because they were being killed.
> I: Who were being killed?
> P: The homosexuals.

Individual economic solvency facilitating independence from familial/kinship obligations has been essential for gay and lesbian identities to become partially public and political in Latin America, as elsewhere (Murray 1995; Carrier 1995; Lumsden 1996; Adam, Duyvendak, and Krouwel 1999). As the economic power of gays in Latin America becomes more visible (through AIDS activism and through the commercialization of sexuality) and neoliberalist values of individualism and consumerism become more generalized, more people may adopt a gay and lesbian identity in Latin America and come out as such. This might unleash homophobic violence, but also decrease the number of unreported, poorly followed, and unpunished crimes. That is, the increasing numbers of hate crimes and other homophobic acts reported in countries such as Honduras might not necessarily reflect an increase in actual cases. As more people come out, it becomes more likely that reports of a homophobic crime will be made by the victims or their friends or relatives. Heretofore, as the Inter-Church Committee on Human Rights in Latin America (ICCHRLA) report noted: "With few exceptions, most of the abuses committed against lesbians and gay men

have gone undocumented and remain shrouded in a blanket of impu-
nity" (ICCHRLA 1996:6). Still, reports from several countries indicate
that the rate of hate crimes is actually on the rise, independent of the
fact that there are more crimes reported than in the past. Thousands of
crimes against transvestites have been reported for Brazil (Mott
1995:225) and the death squads of Mexico, Colombia (Mirken
1995:34), and Chile (NACLA Report on the Americas 1998) against
homosexual people are a relatively recent phenomenon. These death
squad crimes should also be seen as part of a larger wave of paramilitary
terrorism occurring as direct consequence of the end of dictatorial military regimes of the 1970s and 1980s and the decline of the Cold War,
which left massive amounts of weapons in the hands of now underemployed men who took as their responsibility the "cleansing" of society
(DeCesare 1998).

The globalization of sexual identity politics

The importance of sexual identity politics in Latin America has
become particularly clear with the campaigns against discriminatory
policy launched by the International Gay and Lesbian Human Rights
Commission (IGLHRC) and the International Lesbian and Gay Association (ILGA) in the 1990s. In spite of all their good and important
work, these organizations have at times been accused by scholars of
being neocolonialist and of being (perhaps unwitting) agents of the
homogenizing trends in globalization, because they have appeared to
impose international guidelines that have not always been properly
contextualized and are not culturally sensitive (Hasbrouck 1996).[4]

In Honduras, the emergence of gay identities not only has been the
product of economic neoliberalism, but also a consequence of the globalization of human rights discourses and rhetoric. It has often been
claimed that "rightist" neoliberalism and "leftist" human rights move-

---

4.   Mohanty, Russo, and Torres (1991) similarly critiqued the international femi-
      nist movement.

ments constitute competing forces in today's power struggles to reach public opinion and create or resist change. That both "opposing" forces have reached Honduras and impacted the sexual identities and politics of its citizens with rather similar consequences is an example of the multiple and contradictory effects of globalization in today's world.

A society that traditionally privileged gender over sexuality and maintained a complex culture of gender hierarchies where masculine males, or *hombres*, enjoyed power over non-men was strongly affected by an international human rights discourse initially brought to Honduras through the writings of Central American activists such as Jacobo Schifter (1989, Schifter and Madrigal Pana 1992). Using a neo-Marxist analysis based on 1960s' radical feminism (Firestone 1970), several authors have argued that it is possible to establish a parallel between the oppression of women and the oppression of "non-men" or homosexual males (Schifter 1989; Leiner 1994; Lumsden 1996:28). The parallel is that women (regardless of their sexual orientation) and homosexual males are oppressed as a group by heterosexual men; the latter being the ones who enforce an "hegemonic" masculinity.

This approach has had an enormous ideological impact on the Latin American gay liberation movements of the 1980s and 1990s. The approach, however, is problematic: by seeing the relations between males of "hegemonic" and "subordinate" masculinities as part of systems and structures of vertical power and oppression, the power and agency that the members of "subordinate" masculinities possess in the re-creation and maintenance of "hegemonic" masculinities tends to be erased.

The paradigm of masculinist oppression in which homosexual males are "forced" to become feminine so they can be dominated as woman-like creatures, is far too simple. Effeminacy in men is always brutally repressed and castigated by family and neighborhood members during the childhood of the *loca*, in the hope that his feminine traits will disappear and the boy will grow to be a masculine man. Only as these boys reach late adolescence and adulthood, people around them more or less give up their attempts to change them into *hombres*.

I am not arguing that there are not *locas* who cultivate effeminacy because of their homosexual identity or feelings. Indeed, I found this to be the case on several occasions. Not only are *locas* marked as homosexual because of their effeminacy, but also they actively mark themselves as feminine beings in order to highlight and announce their sexual availability to other men. I found the latter, however, to be more of a strategic afterthought in already effeminate men who desire to seduce a "real" man: an *hombre*, who in the fantasy of the *loca*, does not want other *hombres* but only womanly partners (i.e., *locas* and biological women). The Honduran view is that (feminine) gender and (homo-)sexuality are one, and it is difficult even with an outsider view of an analytical distinction between gender and sexuality to suggest the primacy of either one, as each reinforces the other, and as (in general), "the dominated apply categories constructed from the point of view of the dominant to the relations of domination, thus making them appear as natural." (Bourdieu 2001:35).

The sexual-identity-politics/liberationist discourse of the international gay and lesbian human rights movement and AIDS activism offers the possibility of liberation to *locas* mostly to the extent that they masculinize themselves or at least give up their desire of coupling with non-homosexual *hombres* (i.e., adopt gay male endogamy in place of gender exogamy which has also been exogamous for identity as homosexual), and embrace neoliberalist middle-class ideals of individualism. How to create a society that will accept homosexual people not by trying to change them into masculine gay clones but by accepting gender nonconformity and the multiple ways of being gay as valid is a difficult question—one that has not been answered by the gay and lesbigay movements in the north (though recent attempts have been made to include transgendered persons in umbrella organizations labeled LGBT and to celebrate "queerness" which in its historical sense has meant gender-deviant).

Elsewhere in the world, "First World" erotica has provided exciting models of masculine men being penetrated and the switching of roles. Such material was not in evidence among the lower-class homosexuals I knew in San Pedro. They did not have access to video players away from other family members or private space in which to conceal "porn." There was some access to gay printed porno. Miguel Angel Lemus dismissed the muscular models at these magazines as being *locas solapadas* or under-covered *locas* rather than consider delinking gender (masculinity) and sexuality (being penetrated).

Many Latin American homosexuals reject the individualist model because it artificially tends to group them into ghettoes apart from their families and mixed friendship networks (see Taylor 1985; Carrier 1985; Arenas 1997; Carrillo 2002), while not giving conscious thought to economic bases of "familialism" (see Murray 1995:33-48). *Locas* might lack long-lasting relationships with *hombres* in comparison with their gay-model counterparts, but many of them certainly enjoy their rich social life at the barrio and have very nurturing families. As Horacio told me:

INTERVIEWER: Why at your age [38] do you still live with your parents?
HORACIO: Oh, because I don't like the loneliness of living alone. I know homosexual people who live alone and I don't like the way they live.
I: How do they live?
H: See, they live alone. Completely alone. This is, uhm, they don't have true friends who visit them. Usually people come and go as if it were their place. I don't like that lifestyle, not that I couldn't handle it, but I don't like its loneliness. I love family life. For me it is essential. There is nothing more beautiful than getting home and knowing that my mother is there; to know that she is waiting for me, that I can chat with her and exchange a few words with my brothers. Sometimes I don't talk to anyone, but I still feel good

just by knowing that family is in the other rooms. They are good people who are not going to harm me. But when you live alone you don't know who is going to enter your home. There are always people with ulterior intentions.

...

I: Don't you think that perhaps you also live with your family because financially you wouldn't be able to do it on your own?
H: Uhm, no. Economically I don't think I have a problem now [of being able to afford a separate household]. It's simply about loneliness. It doesn't have to do with finances.

The tension between paternalism and liberalism

The tension between paternalism and liberalism when one is working with the Other is evident throughout this book. Trying to "liberate" my representation of homosexuality in Honduras from paternalistic rhetoric that depicts *locas* as victims of structures of domination, I opted for a more pluralist view that looked for agency and autonomy among the people I studied. Therefore, in my language, I moved from "false consciousness" to "agency" and to the relativity of self-representation. Likewise, I preferred "normative" instead of "hegemonic," "alternative" rather than "subordinate," and thought in terms of "power" rather than "oppression," "practices" and "discourse" instead of "structure." As I was presenting my case, however, the inevitability of having to think in terms of oppression became evident. A clear example of oppression is the gendered hierarchization that gives privilege to masculine men by creating compulsory passivity in *locas* and limiting the economic survival of transgender people to perilous street prostitution. The tension here remains unresolved, because the very language of oppression and inequality needed to describe this situation, easily can slip into universalist rhetoric that essentializes the Other and creates further paternalist relationships of dependence.

The paternalism of international development, health, and human rights organizations, with their corresponding local NGOs, continues to prescribe universal standards of ethics, equality, recognition, and liberation from oppression; and to foster the universal implementation of these standards. A unilateral monologue is established where the needs of the "local" are no longer heard. Another problem with paternalism is that by centering its discourse on issues of universal standards it conceals the creators of these very discourses, who most times are not the local people purportedly represented. In facing this dilemma, we ought to ask, who sets the standards and for what purposes?

In the case of economic liberalism, transnational corporations and neoliberal policies also fail in representing the local. Their promotion of cultural relativity and personal specificity has nothing to do with the needs of the local, but with the invisible gaze of those who profit. There is dialogue, but it is a self-interested and deceitful one.

The main paradox about paternalism and liberalism is that despite being so different and presenting themselves as almost contrary to each other, they both create relationships of dependence between the privileged and the Other. Paternalism does it in an overt and more monitorable way. Liberalism works in obscure ways and its maneuvers are difficult to trace. Moreover, as paternalist organizations neoliberalize, the differences between paternalism and liberalism become less evident and tend to blur.

To create dependence, both paternalism and liberalism have to be constructed on some common premises. The first premise is that there is an imagined, more modern world, which is "better" than a less modern one. It is imperative that the more modern world be emulated, so eventually, in a future time a similarly modern status can be attained by those viewed as being currently backward and benighted. Belief in the progress/evolution tale comes across in the "yet" and the "still," and the lacking-of-something in some Hondurans descriptions of situations in Honduras, e.g., Cariaco saying:

> I am still not used to living my sexuality more openly. The homosexual environment of my country still absorbs me. I can't live my sexuality as openly as people do in other countries where they can

have sexual relations with other gays without having to fall into masculine or feminine roles.

As his gay organization struggles to become a recognized component of the international gay and lesbian movement, Cariaco makes it clear that he is working to modernize Honduras so it could resemble more closely the more modern world where gays have a better life:

> We have offered courses of gay consciousness-raising to help homosexuals get rid of their internalized homophobia and to help them adapt a little better to the new and revolutionary ideas [about homosexuality] that have been going on [for some time] in other countries, while our country has been left behind.

Very often it seems necessary to bring people from the "more advanced" countries to tell locals how things are "supposed" to be. Nina Cobos, one of the founders of Prisma, a Tegucigalpa-based group, declares:

> Prisma [is] a social space with some educational character, in the line of working for personal consciousness, self-esteem, and trying to inject a little gay pride in the community. We have done several activities: someone from New York came to share with us his experience of coming out of the closet, what this has meant for him, and his activism among different groups in New York. He is a North American. We also organized a panel to discuss issues related to AIDS. The panel included a sociologist who works in prevention campaigns against AIDS with the Latin American community in Los Angeles and a Honduran physician who had had some experience working with AIDS patients. We also brought a person living with full-blown AIDS from Costa Rica. We wanted to hear his testimony, because we couldn't find anyone here in Honduras who was willing to give a public testimony.

Likewise, a lesbian couple living in the US has worked with locals to start a group for women in Honduras:

The personal consciousness group was born among some women who had been trying to do something in that line for years. A Honduran and her North American partner [both who live in Albuquerque, New Mexico], tried to start the group on several occasions, but with no good results.

The second premise is that there needs to be community leaders with whom nongovernmental organizations (NGOs) can work.[5] Through a long and painful process of depersonalization and repersonalization, local people are told who they are, what to do, and how to do things. As Evelio Pineda, the director of "Proyecto Hombres" explains,

[We formed] as an initiative of the international office of AIDS in Washington, DC. We received funding to develop a program...with four basic aspects...[the third one being] a pro-sustainability program to give life to the program and to energize the gay community per se...

The very name of the project—"Proyecto Hombres"—is symptomatic of the situation of paternalism described. Using "*hombres*" reflects a lack of understanding of more traditional Honduran gender/sexuality systems by excluding, misrepresenting, or marginalizing anyone who does not fit within the traditional *hombre* category.

The politics of authenticity

As Proyecto Hombres struggled to remain viable and fundable by grant-awarding international AIDS prevention agencies, the most vital question gradually shifted from "What do we need?" to "What do **they** want to hear that we need"? This makeover is accomplished by "forgetting" their old baggage and "discovering" who they "really" are. Their "true selves"—who they "really are—then, correspond to the pre-fabri-

---

5.   Just as colonial expropriations required "chiefs" to legitimate expropriating treaties, and often conjured and invested them.

cated image that these international granting agencies had already envisioned, either because these are the type of people whom they are accustomed to funding and "working with" (controlling), or have proved to "work" in a successful funding formula, producing predictable results that will please the funding sources of these agencies.

Paradoxically, these granting agencies do indeed want to fund the "authentically" local and do not perceive that by their very imposition of guidelines and the relationships of dependence that they establish with the local, they are constructing a "local" which they will eventually fund and help to grow and develop in its new form. As Evelio says, "Through this KAP [Knowledge, Attitude, Practice] survey we will know which our weakest areas are."

In 1997 I was asked to give my opinion about a another KAP study on HIV, this time carried out by the United Nations Population Fund in Honduras (Fernández-Alemany 1999). Because of the wording of the survey, the organization came up with the results they wanted to hear and that would enable them to implement their program as smoothly and with minimal changes from the original format imported from the US. In one of the first questions of this UN-KAP survey, people were asked whether they were homosexual or not. The percentage of people self-declared as homosexual was equated with a supposed percentage of homosexual relations in the population studied, assuming that homosexual relations were practiced only and necessarily by people self-identified as homosexual. The analysis, which was performed by highly paid international UN consultants who knew nothing about the Honduran sexuality/gender system, missed the essential point that homosexual identity does not imply sexual activity and also the well-known fact that many people who would not identify as homosexual in a survey **do** recurrently engage in homosexual behavior.

The study also mistakenly created an inverse correlation between degree of religiosity and chance to get an STD, by assuming honesty in answers, disregarding well-known Catholic double standards. That those reporting themselves to be religious reported lower STD rates than those who did not consider themselves religious cannot be taken at face value (as having face validity); it seems likely that religious Catholics under-report STD more than those for whom Catholicism is unimportant.

The relationships of power and dependence created through the funding process are quite clear and affect any possible result or outcome in "quick and dirty" surveys. "We have this project for two years" Dereck, from Proyecto Hombres, declares. "Depending on the results, they will fund us for two more years—"

The power of constructing authenticity lies in the ability of the local to foresee what the funding agency will want to fund and then claim that pre-approved construction as genuinely "local." The process is subtle and dialectic: by the constant circulation of feedback, both the funding agency and the anointed locals gradually erase the evidence of the funding agency's construction of the local, rendering the new and appropriately fundable face of the local as authentic. Thus, an alternative view to the paternalistic model would be that local and global are constantly constructing each other, in constant negotiation and in a continual power flow.[6] Of course, the tension between paternalism and liberalism will continue to exist for as long as there are differences in the accumulation of capital between the "global" and the "local," between "us" and the "Other."

Conclusion

The promise of liberation and consumption brought by human rights and neoliberalist rhetoric, respectively, is predominantly directed at masculine homosexual men, such as *tracas* and some *hombre-hombres*,

6.   I owe this insight to a fertile discussion generated at the roundtable to which I was invited by Charles L. Briggs, "The new rush to the 'local': Transnational interests in producing local subjects," at the 2000 annual meeting of the Law and Society Association in Miami.

who in the past had not been able to come to terms with their sexuality precisely because their masculine gender self-identity and self-presentation did not fit within a sexual culture in which only effeminate men are considered to be "homosexuals." This sector of masculine gay men is the one that most benefits from the importing and appropriating "modern" (American) gay identity. Increased consciousness of the problematic effects of neoliberalism and the globalization of human rights and AIDS activism rhetoric is essential if these locally emerging gay movements are to make sense of their conflicting meanings of "gay" and decrease rather than enhance gender inequality within their sexual cultures.[7]

---

7.   Some of the problematic effects of neoliberalism can be summarized as: the invisibility of power, oppressive labor politics and the dehumanization of the workplace due to mobility, the constant change of the workplace, and job instability, and an explicit exploitation of work force facilitated by the intangibility of profit (Nash and Fernández-Kelly 1983).

10

CONCLUSIONS

I began this research not only before the (1998) publication of Prieur's and Kulick's studies of transvestite prostitutes in Mexico and Brazil, but before (1995) publication of the books by Carrier and Murray on (primarily) Mesoamerica. What I observed in the field in San Pedro de Sula is traditional, lower-class heterogender homosexuality, some of the assumptions of which also characterize the relations between transvestite prostitutes and their lovers (*maridos* or *novios*) described by Prieur and Kulick and the Latin American *ambiente* of the pre-AIDS era in which Carrier and Murray began their research.

Like the transvestites whom Kulick and Prieur interviewed, the effeminate (but not transvestite) homosexuals of San Pedro are demurely unphallic, often covering their genitals as their anuses are penetrated by phallic/masculine young men who do not consider themselves to be "homosexual" even if all their sexual relations are with biological males. Although they may hide them in deference to the heterosexual self-image of their sexual partners, the penetrated homosexuals do not want their male genitalia excised (nor did the transvestite prostitutes studied by Kulick and Prieur). Couplings, whether they last a few minutes or a few years, are between "men" and "homosexuals" (*hombres* and *locas*). That is, the pairings are exogamous in gender/sexual orientation, these analytically distinct categories being a unity in the understanding of both the "men" and the male homosexual unmen. The cultural belief of "naturally" different penetrators and penetratees is sufficiently strong that neither *locas* nor their *hombre* partners seek recourse to surgery to transform the effeminate males into females. Wherever their dispositions (in the Bourdieuian sense of *habitus*) originated, *locas* actively mark (and market) themselves as feminine in order to attract penetrators. Meanwhile, the "naturalness" of the men's masculinity is questioned neither by the men nor by their sexual partners who desire masculine sexual partners and are heavily invested in the view of their penetrators as completely masculine.

"Topping" those who seek to be "topped" does **not** enhances the masculine honor of the men who penetrate homosexuals. Although not as bashful as the "husbands" supported by transgendered males in Brazil or Mexico, or among the traditional Chukchi of Siberia (Bogoras 1904), the young *hombres* whom I interviewed did not brag to their neighbors or family members about their "conquests" of homosexuals, or even about the benefits they squeezed out of homosexuals as tribute to their phallic superiority. Even though they obey the mandate to penetrate and never to be penetrated, the *hombres* are aware that they are engaged in somewhat suspect conduct, even if neither they nor others defined what they do as "homosexuality" or "prostitution" (see Cáceres and Jiménez 1999:191 on similar hiding from those not *de ambiente* the knowledge that young Peruvian males are penetrating males). At best, the masculine honor of those penetrating male bodies is unaffected by what they do to homosexual males.[1]

The *hombre*'s impenetrability is a concern of his homosexual partner who wants to be with a particularly splendid example of the prey "real man" and who loses face if the *hombre completo* (whom the homosexual brags to their friend only strays from women to penetrate one homosexual) engages in sex with other homosexual males. Even more mortifying for the homosexual is to learn from a snickering rival that one's penetrator (whose masculinity one has lauded to other homosexuals) has been penetrated by someone. Worst of all is to learn that someone

---

1.   Similar conclusions that discreet, compartmentalized involvement in penetrating males neither increases nor decreases honor have been reached by Carrier 1995:16, 198; Murray 1995:53-55; Arboleda 1997; Prieur 1998:188-89, 196-97; and Green 1999:187.

who one believed was *un hombre completo* has been penetrated by a *loca*. Despite the widely credited "naturalness" of the dichotomization of males into homosexuals and *hombres*, such "horrifying" behavior occurs (though, perhaps less often than rival *locas* claim).

Many of those who seek to be penetrated are quite unashamed about getting what they want—which is not "masculine honor," or, for that matter, the "feminine honor" of demure, sexually frigid mothers. The Honduran *obvios* are not just unashamed of being penetrated by masculine men, but delighted and eager to recount the details of the experience of being well-fucked by masculine men. Whereas *activos* (unless disinhibited by alcohol and/or drugs, as in the cantina encounter) are skittish about discussing or even admitting to having sex with males, *obvios* are "shameless" in the view of the majority culture and of their partners who don't want their association with homosexuals known to others. Many of those worshipped as hypermasculine by the males they penetrate come across as being ashamed to have it known that they have sex with males, while their purportedly "dishonored" partners enthusiastically discuss (within the *ambiente* and to a sympathetic foreign ethnographer) what should shame them **if** they aspired to be considered men. Some even foment "scandal," stirring up masculine-heterosexual potential partners who seem to be ignoring their availability and attractiveness. Abashed insertors and proud receptors is what one sees on the ethnographic ground (in Honduras, as elsewhere in Latin America) of males who have sex with males, not the "subject honor, object shame" deducible from the dominant culture's abstract values elicited from those not engaged in male-male sex.[2]

In the Weberian definition of power as getting what one wants despite resistance (Weber 1978:53), it is the homosexual who carries out his will despite the reluctance of the men. The homosexuals are penetrated, but it is their phallus-wielding, masculine partners who are, in effect, passive instruments doing what the less masculine males

2. See Wikan's (1984) challenge to "shame" being the obverse of "honor."

want, and attaining less pleasure (or at least less acknowledged pleasure) than the homosexuals take from their physical unions. The homosexuals contend that they are in control, getting what they want, while their *hombre* partners would prefer not to talk about or think perspectives from which they look passive, objectified, and used by the unmasculine males who rent the pride and symbol of young men's masculinity.

Even in the Foucaultian notion of "governance" as organizing and orchestrating the settings in which human interactions occur, it is the desires and the ideology of the *locas* that sets the terms of engagement. Both *hombres* and *locas* believe that they are in control, but such beliefs are epiphenomenal in the Foucaultian view. Indeed, the illusion of agency and choice (by any and, even more, by all parties) fits well with Foucault's worldview. My project herein has been Weberian (*verstehensoziologie*) in seeking to investigate the meanings that action hold for the acting individual and in not viewing people simply as products of social forces and subservient to received cultural structurings or victimized by "false consciousness." As the late Eric Wolf (1999:8) wrote, "It is part of the ethnographer's task to bring together the different pronouncements, to note their congruence or disjunction, to test them against other things said and done, and to guess at what they might be about." In this book, I have brought together the only partly complementary understandings of homosexual-*hombre* relations of the homosexuals and of the *hombres* involved in a large Honduran city. Although discourse has consequences for shaping the conduct of relations and relationships, "behavior often fails to follow the scripts laid out in discourses and texts," as Wolf also noted (18). Moreover, there is some diversity of cultural rules, as well as a diversity of behavior (48), and if there is any pain from cognitive dissonance, most people bear it easily—and unconsciously.[3]

Preserving a record of a possibly vanishing lifeway?

The cultural model of heterogender (homo)sexuality has been durable in circum-Mediterranean societies and in former colonies of Iberian states. It remains to be seen whether it will persist in competition with the new and alien categorization of insertors as (also being) "homosexual." Both the modern gay model from the prestigious countries to the north and the rigorist codes of Mormon and fundamentalist Protestant congregations—which were also sponsored by missionaries from the north and are booming in Central America (see Brusco 1995)—treat insertors and insertees as instances of the same ontological category "homosexual." Both the *norteño* pro-gay (and often gay) advisors on preventing HIV prevention—including those seeking to save bodies through gay community-building—and the *norteño* Protestant missionaries who see themselves as saving souls by discouraging nonmarital sex share a view of Latino culture(s) as backward, benighted, and hypocritical; see themselves as advocates of honesty and personal responsibility, and seeing personal responsibility as the royal road to prosperity and salvation. Neoliberal economics of the body is spreading along with neoliberal macroeconomic measures and the old economy of gendered homosexuality may disappear.

I was certainly not doing "salvage anthropology" in the sense of eliciting accounts of what life used to be like in the San Pedro *ambiente*. However, in the sense of recording the culture of a particular time and place, sound ethnography always has a quality of preserving what quickly become "historical" records of what people did and thought (see Gleach 2002).

---

3. "Not all people are equally concerned with creating cognitive coherence. , , , The readiness of many people to live with contradictions, as well as the proclivity of most to pay little heed to internal cognitive coherence, suggests that installation of a vision of cosmic order is more likely to be an imperative for those trying to organize power [including alien ethnographers as well as of sociopolitical entrepreneurs] than the reflection of a general striving for cognitive consistency" (Wolf 1999:56, 290).

The structuring of the San Pedro *ambiente* of the late-1990s may not be eternal, though it certainly appears consistent with reports of the traditional sexual culture from earlier studies of Latin American *ambientes*. Bourdieu (2001), while insisting that the structures of domination are historical—the products of an incessant (and therefore historical) labour of reproduction" (34), represented the "traditional" Mediterranean structure of masculine domination as only being superficially altered in postmodern France. Masculinity in sexualized relations to nonmasculinity is continuing to be reproduced in San Pedro and elsewhere and engaging in while rejecting being defined by same-sex sexual relations occurs in the First-World "gay Meccas," not just among masculine-defined penetrators in such peripheries of the global economy as Honduras.

Postscript

That, insofar as things have changed since my fieldwork, they have changed for the worse is indicated by March 2002 news reports of police crackdowns in San Pedro Sula following the inauguration of President Ricardo Maduro (27 January). San Pedro Mayor Oscar Kilgore ordered the arrest of any transvestites of any "transvestite and effeminate-looking people" daring to cross the railroad tracks the separate the city's south side from downtown. This "cleansing" is a part of Maduro's "zero tolerance for crime and delinquency" initiative

Prior to Maduro' taking office, Mayor Kilgore ordered a raid on the city's only gay bar, "Boys," on January 12th. Twelve people including Comunidad Gay staff members and its director, Jorge Flores were arrested and held for 24 hours before being released without charged being filed. The bar remained closed. Also, the government has announced the formation of a "reeducation" program for prostitutes, and several transvestites as well as female prostitutes have been transported and involuntarily enrolled.

Municipal Judge Alvaro Aguilar Frenzel denied the group's allegations regarding the bar raid, claiming that no one has been arrested in bar raids and that the only arrests on record have taken place in the street in downtown San Pedro Sula. "We have people eating dinner with their children in restaurants who have complained to the police department about nearly naked men dressed as women on the street trying to sell their bodies," said Frenzel. However, there documentation related to 27 arrests that were made on First Avenue in downtown San Pedro Sula 24 April 2001, based on a law against offending "public morality." (ILGHRC Action Alert, 13 March 2002).

ACKNOWLEDGEMENTS

Manuel Fernández-Alemany: I am grateful to "Proyecto HON/96/ P01-II del Fondo de Población de las Naciones Unidas" (United Nations Population Fund in Honduras), especially Erika Bernhard y Arie Hoekman for providing me with office space, computers and Internet during my fieldwork of 1997. Thanks, too, to Licenciado Juan Ramón Gradelhy R., director of the AIDS institution COMVIDA in San Pedro Sula and to Licenciado Carlos Eduardo Gallegos Figueroa, director at that time of the Centro Universitario Regional del Norte in San Pedro Sula, for supporting my research in its initial stages. My fieldwork would have not been possible without the tremendous help and support of both Jesús Guillén, president of the Asociación Hondureña de Homosexuales y Lesbianas Contra el Sida, and his mother, Doña Felícita Salguero, who let me stay in their home and fed me well each of the many times I had a financial crisis I also would have not completed my fieldwork had not Dereck G. Raickov, director of the NGO Comunidad Gay Sampedrana provided me with his full support, access to computers and Internet, and very importantly, access to several bisexual men who otherwise I would have not been able to interview during my fieldwork of 1998. I am immensely grateful to Dereck and to the men who let me interview them and whose names I have changed in the text. I am also very grateful to the library staff of the Centro Cultural Sampedrano who patiently assisted me in the search of material and saw me almost everyday coming to work in their library; they took good care of my materials when I left them unattended and even let me in with my water bottle!

Many thanks as well to the Institute for the Study of Human Resources for a Hal Call Mattachine Scholarship award to complete my dissertation; the Dorothy Leonard Fund at the University of

Southern California for sponsoring the still photograph project "Stories about masculinity," which made my fourth and final trip to Honduras in 1998 possible; the USC Lambda Alumni Association Research Scholarship which partially funded my 1997 trip to Honduras; the USC Center for Feminist Research for a travel grant to Honduras in 1996; and a Rockefeller Foundation postdoctoral fellowship which underwrote a year at the University of California, San Diego Ethnic Studies Department to work with Ramón Guttiérez and Charles Briggs.

My special and melancholic feelings of gratitude go to Miguel Ángel Lemus and Isidro Romero, both now deceased due to complications related to AIDS, who taught me so much about the sexual cultures in San Pedro Sula.

In her seminar on feminist issues in anthropology Nancy C. Lutkehaus recognized the theoretical importance of my research and encouraged me to further advance it. I also thank her for the careful editorial work she did on my dissertation. I wish to thank G. Alexander Moore, Chair of the Anthropology Department at USC and member of my dissertation committee for his enormous support throughout my Ph.D. studies and his always wise advice. I am also very grateful to Michael A. Messner, member of my dissertation committee at USC, for his important feedback and inspiring insights in the study of masculinities.

Finally, I am forever grateful to Dr. Walter L. Williams, PhD advisor and Chair of my dissertation committee for his consistent support and mentoring at many different levels and close guidance throughout my studies. I benefited tremendously from his seminar on gay and lesbian studies and politics and his lectures on how to reduce prejudice, heterosexism, and homophobia. I also thank him for his editorial work on my dissertation and other writings.

My very special thanks to Stephen O. Murray, Eric C. Graham, Gloria González-López, Gordon Glor, Jay Hasbrouck, Adriene Pine, and Ildiko Tenyi for the countless hours spent reading my work and their fantastic and challenging editorial job and influence they have had on my writing during my years of postgraduate studies. I feel immensely fortunate of having had the unlimited support and mentoring of Dr. Murray throughout my studies and the in taking over turning my dissertation into a book. I also wish to thank European scholars Gert Hekma and Annick Prieur for their sharp and valuable comments on drafts of dissertation chapters.

I would like to thank the following people for their support during my American studies and Honduran fieldwork: Gaelyn Aguilar, Dennis Altman, Karen Aragon, Lourdes Argüelles, Armida Ayala, Peter Biella, James Bigelow, Joseph Carrier, Héctor Carrillo, Nina Cobos, Hernán Cruz, Wendy DeBoer, Steven Epstein, Irene Fertik, Edward Finegan, Manolo Flores, Tim Frasca, Miguel García, Elan Glasser, Gillian Goslinga, Judith Grant, Don Julio Guillén, Joseph Hawkins, Gilbert Herdt, Adriana Hernández, Geovanny Hernández, Mike Hickey, Peter Jackson, Rita R. Jones, Don Kulick, Roger Lancaster, Esdras Leitao, Peter Levine, Alonso López, Óscar Mejía, Luiz Mott, Peter Nardi, Irma Palma, George Patton, Guillermo Reyes, Dena Saxer, Andrei Simic, Michael Stevenson, Manolo Ríos Tavarone, John Richards, Barbara Robinson, Grace Rosales, Marco Ruiz, Andrés Sciolla, Alissa Simon, Carl Totton, Ferry Heiman Urbach, Miguel Valle, and Todd White.

Stephen Murray: I am grateful to scholars and editors who have, over the years, encouraged my research on Latin American male homosexualities: Barry Adam, Manuel Arboleda G., Ralph Bolton, Joseph Carrier, Héctor Carrillo, Wayne Dynes, David Greenberg, Dwight Heath, Guillermo Hernández Ch., Badruddin Khan, Bill Leap, Heather McClure, Luiz Mott, Peter Nardi, the late Kenneth Payne, Luiz Diaz-Perdomo, Ken Plummer, Will Roscoe, Clark Taylor, Pablo Tellez, Fred Whitam, Walter Williams, Wayne Wooden; to Niyi Akinnaso, Keith Basso, John Gumperz, Paul Kay, Don Kulick, the late Jesse Sawyer, Amparo Tusón, and the late Florence Voegelin, for encouraging me to undertake an ethnography of gay speaking; and, most of all, to my life partner, Keelung Hong, who has been a patient traveling companion to various Latin American ports of call during the last two-plus decades, including during the incursion into Honduras that never officially happened.

The cover photo, showing the *hombre* gaze on a city street is presented without any knowledge of the sexual conduct of the young men. It was shot by Manuel Arboleda G., to whom we are grateful for permission to reproduce it here.

GLOSSARY OF TERMS

armas al hombro = missionary position, but the bottom has both legs on the shoulders of the top

bolo = drunk

bordo = the border of the river and of the colony

buitre = "straight" man interested in sex with *locas* in exchange for a gift or money

candelita chorreada = one sitting on the other

changoneta = in a joking fashion; not taking things too seriously

chapuline = literally, locust ; predatory hustler-thieves in Mexico and Costa Rica

chava = adolescent girl

chele = light skin, white, or blond

choz or **chocero** = robber, from *"chocear"*, to steal, and this from *choza* (hut) implying perhaps that robbers live in huts

cipote = teenager

colectivo = like a taxi, but with a fixed itinerary and which takes up to 5 passengers besides the driver

colorinche = a person with color or who da color (see entry "dar color")

cómputo = the Spanish version of *raga* or rap-reggae, coming mainly from Panamá, where El General is its most important representative

cuadrado = squared; *hombres* who are not buitres; cuadrados are *hombres* who are not in *ambiente*

culero = faggot; from "culo" (ass)

dar color = literally, to give color to someone or to color someone up. It means to make someone obviously homosexual because of his proximity to someone who is too obvious. In other countries, as in Chile and Mexico, to "burn" someone has a similar meaning

gringo/a = a white person from the United States. Sometimes is also used for white people from commonwealth countries and northern European countries.

hombre = in regard to sex, male; in regard to gender, masculine

jetelear = give blow jobs

loca = literally, crazy girl; effeminate, penetrated homosexual male

mara = gang

marinovios = a combination marido (husband) and novio (fiancé)

mariquera = money in exchange for sex. It comes from Marta, a woman's name that in this case stands for Sugar-Mommie

mayate = literally, dung beetle; masculine young men (diffused from Mexico, known to some in San Pedro)

nachos = corn chips

novia = regular girlfriend

piropo = a flirtatious and embellished remark, usually cried out loud in the public from a man to a woman, but sometimes from an *hombre* to a *loca*

ponerla = to put a knife on someone, meaning to rob someone

popsicle = HIV+; someone with AIDS

rebanar = joking, though literally, "cutting in pieces"

solapa = closeted gay

tortillear or **hacer tortillas** = having sex with another passive, *loca*

travesti = male dressing as a female (without the fetishistic sense of the clinical term)

trigueño = dark-skinned

trinca = kisses

BIBLIOGRAPHY

Abreu, Caio Fernando. 1983. "Sergeant Garcia." In *My deep dark pain is love: A collection of Latin American fiction,* ed. by Winston Leyland, 267-77. San Francisco: Gay Sunshine Press.

Abu-Lughod, Lila. 1991. Writing against culture. In *Recapturing Anthropology,* ed. by Richard Fox, 137-62. Santa Fe: School of American Research Press.

Adam, Barry D. 1978. *The survival of domination.* New York: Elsevier.

—. 1985. Age, structure, and sexuality: Reflections on the anthropological evidence on homosexual relations. *Journal of Homosexuality* 11:19-33.

—. 1993. In Nicaragua: Homosexuality without a gay world. *Journal of Homosexuality* 24:171-81.

Adam, Barry D., Jan Willem Duyvendak, and André Krouwel. 1999. *The global emergence of gay and lesbian politics: National imprints of a worldwide movement.* Philadelphia: Temple University Press.

Aggleton, Peter, ed. 1999. *Men who sell sex: International perspectives on male prostitution and HIV/AIDS.* Philadelphia: Temple University Press.

Altman, Dennis. 1982. *The Americanization of the homosexual, the homosexualization of America.* New York: St. Martin's Press.

—. 1996. Rupture or continuity?: The internationalization of gay identities. *Social Text* 48:77-94.

—. 1997 Global gays/ global gaze. *GLQ* 3:417-36.

Arboleda G., Manuel. 1995. Social attitudes and sexual variance in Lima. In Murray (1995:100-10).

—. 1997. On some of Lancaster's misrepresentations. *American Ethnologist* 24:931-34.

Arenas, Reinaldo. 1993. *Before night falls.* New York: Viking.

Argüelles, Lourdes, and Manuel Fernández-Alemany. 1997. Working with *heterosexismo* in Latino/a immigrant Los Angeles. In *Overcoming heterosexism and homophobia: Strategies that work*, ed. by James T. Sears and Walter L. Williams. New York: Columbia University Press,

Bech, Henning. 1997. *When men meet: Homosexuality and modernity.* Chicago: University of Chicago Press.

Berlin, Brent. 1992. *Ethnobiological classification.* Princeton, NJ: Princeton Univ. Press.

Bernard, H. Russell, and Jesús Salinas Pedraza. 1989. *Native Ethnography: A Mexican Indian describes his own culture.* Newbury Park, CA: Sage.

Bogoras, Waldemar G. 1904. *The Chukchee.* American Museum of Natural History Memoir ll, 2.

Bolton, Ralph. 1992. Mapping terra incognita: Sex research for AIDS prevention—an urgent agenda for the 1990s. In *The time of AIDS: Social analysis, theory, and method*, ed. by Gilbert Herdt and Shirley Lindenbaum. Newbury Park, CA: Sage, pp. 124-158.

—. 1994. Sex, science, and social responsibility: Cross-cultural research on same-sex eroticism and sexual intolerance. *Cross-cultural research* 28:134-90.

Boster, James S. 1985. Requiem for "the omniscient informant": "There's life in the old girl yet". In *New directions in cognitive anthropology* ed. by Janet Dougherty. Urbana: University of Illinois Press, pp. 77-97.

—. 1986. Exchange of varieties and information between Aguaruna manioc cultivators. *American Anthropologist* 88:428-36.

Bourdieu, Pierre. 1992. *Outline of a theory of practice*. New York: Cambridge University Press.

—. 2001. *Masculine Domination*. Cambridge: Polity Press.

Bowman, Kirk S. 1999. Taming the tiger in Honduras. *LASA Forum* 33 (1):9-12.

Brandes, Stanley 1981. Like wounded stags: Male sexual ideology in an Andalusian town. In *Sexual meanings: The cultural construction of gender and sexuality*, ed. by Sherry B. Ortner and Harriet Whitehead. New York: Cambridge University Press, pp. 216-39.

Briggs, Charles L. 1986. *Learning how to ask: A sociolinguistic appraisal of the role of the interview in social science research*. New York: Cambridge University Press.

Brown, Stephen. 1999. Democracy and sexual difference: the lesbian and gay movement in Argentina. In Adam et al. (1999:110-32).

Brusco, Elizabeth E. 1995. *The reformation of machismo: Evangelical conversion and gender in Colombia*. Austin: University of Texas Press.

Burdick, J. Alan, and Stewart D. Yvette. 1974. Differences between the "show" and "no show" volunteers in a homosexual population. *Journal of Social Psychology* 92:159-60.

Bustos-Aguilar, Pedro. 1995. "Mister, don't touch the banana": Notes on the popularity of the ethnosexed body south of the border. *Critique of Anthropology* 15:149-70.

Butler, Judith P. 1990. *Gender trouble: Feminism and the subversion of identity.* New York: Routledge.

—. 1993. *Bodies that matter: On the discursive limits of "sex."* New York: Routledge.

Cáceres, Carlos F. 1996. *Sexual cultures and sexual health among young people in Lima in the 1900s.* Doctoral dissertation, University of California at Berkeley.

Cáceres, Carlos F., and Oscar G. Jiménez. 1999. *Fletes* in Parque Kennedy: Sexual cultures among young men who sell sex to other men in Lima. In Aggleton (1999:179-93.)

Cáceres, Carlos F. and Ana María Rosasco. 1999. The margin has many sides: Diversity among gay and homosexually active men in Lima. *Culture, Health & Sexuality* 1:261-75.

Carballo-Diéguez, Alex. 1989. Hispanic culture, gay male culture, and AIDS. *Journal of Counseling and Development* 68:26-30.

Carballo-Diéguez, Alex, and Curtis Dolezal. 1993. Contrasting types of Puerto Rican men who have sex with men (MSM). *Journal of Psychology & Human Sexuality* 6 (4):41-67.

Carrier, Joseph. 1976. Cultural factors affecting urban Mexican homosexual behavior. *Archives of Sexual Behavior* 5:103-14.

—. 1985. Mexican male bisexuality. *Journal of Homosexuality* 11 (1/2):75-85.

—. 1995. *De los otros: Intimacy and homosexuality among Mexican men.* New York: Columbia University Press.

—. 1999. Reflections on ethical problems encountered in field research on Mexican male homosexuality: 1968 to present. *Culture, Health & Sexuality* 1:207-21.

—. 2000. Review of Kulick (1998), Prieur (1998), Schifter (1998). *Journal of Gay & Lesbian Social Services* 11 (4):119-25.

Carrillo, Héctor. 1999. Cultural change, hybridity and male homosexuality in Mexico. *Culture, Health & Sexuality* 1(3):223-38.

—. 2002. *"The night is young": Sexuality in Mexico in the time of AIDS*. Chicago: University of Chicago Press.

Chauncey, George Jr., 1993. *Gay New York: Gender, urban culture, and the makings of the gay male world, 1890-1940*. New York: Basic Books.

Collinson, David L. 1995[1988]. "Engineering humour": Masculinity, joking and conflict in shop-floor relations. In *Men's lives* (3rd edition), ed. by Michael S. Kimmel and Michael A. Messner. Boston: Allyn and Bacon, pp. 164-75.

Comstock, Gary David. 1991. *Violence against lesbians and gay men*. New York: Columbia University Press.

de Beauvoir, Simone. 1978[1949]. *The second sex*. New York: Knopf.

DeCesare, Donna. 1998. The children of war: Street gangs in El Salvador. *NACLA Report on the Americas* 32 (1):21-29.

Derrida, Jacques. 1988[1977]. "Signature event context." In *Limited, Inc.*, ed. by Gerald Graff. Evanston, IL: Northwestern University Press, pp. 1-23.

Díaz, Rafael M. 1998. *Latino gay men and HIV: Culture, sexuality, and risk behavior*. New York: Routledge.

DIEM/FNUAP. 1996. *Encuesta estándar sobre población e indicadores socio-económicos, 1995, EPIS'95: Aspectos metodológicos, Tomo I.* San Pedro Sula: DIEM/FNUAP, pp. 54-55.

Donaldson, Mike. 1993. What is hegemonic masculinity? *Theory and Society* 22:643-57.

Dundes, Alan, with Marcelo M. Suárez-Orozco. 1987. The *piropo* and the dual image of women in the Spanish-speaking world. In *Parsing through customs: Essays by a Freudian folklorist,* by Alan Dundes. Madison: University of Wisconsin Press, pp. 118-44.

Edelman, Lee. 1994. *Homographesis: Essays in gay literary and cultural theory,* by Lee Edelman. New York: Routledge.

Elliott, Richard. 1995. Homophobia in Latin America. *Americas Update* 17 (1):1-3.

—. 1996a. *Human rights violations in Honduras against sexual minorities and people with HIV/AIDS.* Prepared with the assistance of CIPRODEH, Tegucigalpa, Honduras and CLAIR, Ottawa, Canada.

—. 1996b. Reporte: Honduras. *ka-buum 7: En Honduras.* (Manuel Fernández-Alemany and Sam Larson, eds.)

Enguix Grau, Begoña. 1996. *Poder y deseo: La homosexualidad* masculina en Valencia. València: Edicions Alfons el Magnànim.

Eyre, Stephen L. 1997. The vernacular term interview: Eliciting social knowledge related to sex among adolescents. *Journal of Adolescence* 20:9-27.

Fernández-Alemany, Manuel. 1995. Honduras: Somos varones homosexuales; entrevista con Osvaldo. Part I: *De Ambiente* 8 (December 1994-January 1995); Part II: *De Ambiente* 9 (February-March 1995), Los Angeles, California.

—. 1997a. Review of Murray (1995). *American Anthropologist* 99:186.

—. 1997b. Tease + contempt = desire?: The macho/*culero* complex. Paper presented in "Forms of Desire" conference, The City University of New York Graduate School and University Center.

—. 2000. Review of Aggleton (1998) and Schifter (1998). *Journal of Sex Research* 37:187-90.

Fernández-Alemany, Manuel, and Sam Larson, eds. 1996. *ka-buum 7: En Honduras.*

Fernández-Alemany, Manuel, and Andrés Sciolla. 1999. *Mariquitas y marimachos: Guía completa de la homosexualidad.* Madrid: Nuer Ediciones.

Figueroa, Faizury. 1993. *El sida en Honduras.* Tegucigalpa: CEDOH.

Firestone, Shulamith. 1970. *The dialectic of sex: The case for feminist revolution.* New York: Quill.

Foucault, Michel. 1978. *The history of sexuality: An introduction, volume I.* New York: Random House.

García Trujillo, Odalys, Mayté Paredes, and Manuel Sierra. 1998. *VIH/SIDA: Análisis de la evolución de la epidemia en Honduras.* Tegucigalpa: Fundación Fomento en Salud.

Gaudio, Rudolf P. 1998. "Male lesbians" and other queer notions in Hausa. In Murray & Roscoe (1998:115-28).

Gilmore, David D. 1990. *Manhood in the making: Cultural concepts of masculinity.* New Haven: Yale University Press.

—. 1996. Above and below: Toward a social geometry of gender. *American Anthropologist* 98:54-66.

Gleach, Frederic W. 2002. Anthropological professionalization and the Virginia Indians at the turn of the century. *American Anthropologist* 104: in press.

Goffman, Erving. 1959. *The presentation of self in everyday life.* Garden City, NY: Doubleday.

Green, James N. 1999. *Beyond carnival: Male homosexuality in twentieth-century Brazil.* Chicago: University of Chicago Press.

Greenberg, David F. 1988. *The construction of homosexuality.* Chicago: University of Chicago Press.

Grupo Editorial. 1989. *Enciclopedia Histórica 11: Gobiernos contemporáneos.* Tegucigalpa: Graficentro Editores.

Gutmann, Matthew. 1996. *The meanings of macho: Being a man in Mexico City.* Berkeley: University of California Press.

Hart, Donn V. 1992 [1968]. The Cebuano bayot and lakin-on. In *Oceanic homosexualities,* by Stephen O. Murray. New York: Garland, pp. 193-230.

Hasbrouck, Jay. 1996. Gay liberation or gay colonization?: Issues and suggestions for the global lesbian, gay, and bisexual movement. Paper presented at the 95th annual meeting of the American Anthropological Association, San Francisco.

Herdt, Gilbert, 1999. *Sambia Sexual Culture.* Chicago: University of Chicago Press.

Hong, Keelung, and Stephen O. Murray. 1989. Complicity with domination. *American Anthropologist* 91:1028-30.

Hymes, Dell H. 1974. *Foundations in sociolinguistics: An ethnographic approach*. Philadelphia: University of Pennsylvania Press.

ICCHRLA (Inter-Church Committee on Human Rights in Latin America). 1996. *Violence unveiled: Repression against lesbians and gay men in Latin America*. (Special Report). Toronto: ICH-HRLA.

Inforpress Centroamericana. 1994. Aids and sexuality in Central America (Special Report). *Central America Report* 21 (24):2-6.

Kay, Paul. 1978. Tahitian words for "race" and "class." *Publications de la Société des Océanistes* 39:81-91.

Klein, Charles. 1998. Gender, sexuality and AIDS prevention in Brazil. *NACLA Report on the Americas* 31 (4):27-32.

Kleinman, Sherryl. 1999. Essaying the personal: making sociological stories stick. In *Qualitative sociology as everyday life*, edited by Berry Glassner and Rosanna Hertz. London: Sage, pp. 19-29.

Kulick, Don. 1996. Causing a commotion: Public scandal as resistance among Brazilian transgendered prostitutes. *Anthropology Today* 12 (6):3-7.

—. 1997. The gender of Brazilian transgendered prostitutes. *American Anthropologist* 99:574-85.

—. 1998a. *Travesti: Sex, gender, and culture among Brazilian transgendered prostitutes*. Chicago: University of Chicago Press.

—. 1998b. "Fe/male trouble": the unsettling place of lesbians in the self-images of Brazilian travesti prostitutes. *Sexualities* 1:299-312.

Kulick, Don, and Margaret Willson. 1995. *Taboo: Identity and erotic subjectivity in anthropological fieldwork*, ed. by Don Kulick New York: Routledge.

Kutsche, Paul. 1995. Two truths about Costa Rica. In Murray (1995:111-37).

Lacan, Jacques. 1977[. *Écrits: A selection*. New York: Norton.

—. 1978. *The four fundamental concepts of psycho-analysis*. New York: Norton.

LaFaye, Jacques. 1976. *Quetzalcoatl and Guadalupe: The formation of Mexican national consciousness, 1531-1813*. Chicago: University of Chicago Press.

Lancaster, Roger N. 1992. *Life is hard: Machismo, danger, and the intimacy of power in Nicaragua*. Berkeley: University of California Press.

Lane, Erskine. 1978. *Game-texts: A Guatemalan journal*. San Francisco: Gay Sunshine Press.

Larvie, Patrick. 1999. Natural-born targets: male hustlers and AIDS prevention in urban Brazil. In Aggleton (1999:159-78).

Leap, William, and Ellen Lewin, eds. 1996. *Out in the field: Reflections of lesbian and gay anthropologists*. Urbana: University of Illinois Press.

Leiner, Marvin. 1994. *Sexual politics in Cuba: Machismo, homosexuality, and AIDS*. Boulder, CO: Westview Press.

Leznoff, Maurice. 1954. *The homosexual in urban society*. M.A. thesis, sociology, McGill University.

—. 1956. Interviewing homosexuals. *American Journal of Sociology* 62:202-04.

Liguori, Ana Luisa, and Peter Aggleton. 1999. Aspects of male sex work in Mexico City. In Aggleton (1999:103-25).

López de Velasco, Juan. 1971[1571-1574]. *Geografía y descripción universal de las Indias Occidentales*. Madrid: Ediciones Atlas.

Lowe, Lisa, and David Lloyd, eds. 1997. *The politics of culture in the shadow of capital*. Durham, NC: Duke University Press.

Lumsden, Ian. 1991. *Homosexuality, society and the state in Mexico*. Toronto: Canadian Gay Archives.

—. 1996. *Machos, maricones, and gays: Cuba and homosexuality*. Philadelphia: Temple University Press.

Lyman, Peter. 1995[1987]. The fraternal bond as a joking relationship: A case study of the role of sexist jokes in male group bonding. In *Men's lives* (3rd edition), ed. by Michael S. Kimmel and Michael A. Messner. Boston: Allyn and Bacon, pp. 86-96.

MacLeod, Murdo. 1973[1520-1720]. *Spanish Central America: A socioeconomic history, 1520-1720*. Berkeley: University of California Press.

Madrigal, Johnny. 1989. ¿Existe la identidad gay en Costa Rica? *Iconoclasta* 2:19-21.

Manalansan, Martin F., IV. 1997. In the shadows of Stonewall: Examining gay transnational politics and the diasporic dilemma. In *The politics of culture in the shadow of capital*, ed. by Lisa Lowe and David Lloyd. Durham, NC: Duke University Press.

Martin, JoAnn. 1990. Motherhood and power: the production of a women's culture of politics in a Mexican community. *American Ethnologist* 17:470-90.

Melhuus, Marit, and Kristi Anne Stølen. 1996. *Machos, mistresses, madonnas: Contesting the power of Latin American gender imagery*. London: Verso.

Merton, Robert K. 1972. Insiders and outsiders. *American Journal of Sociology* 77:9-47.

Mirandé, Alfredo. 1997. *Hombres y machos: Masculinity and Latino culture.* Boulder, CO: Westview Press.

Mirken, Bruce. 1995. The "undesirable" activist: A gay Colombian takes on death squads. *Frontiers* (April 21):34.

Morales, Marlon I. 1997. Submitting or resisting: Exploring the popular Central American belief that homosexuality can be induced. Www.geocities.com/WestHollywood/2874/anthro134. html

Morton, Helen. 1995. My "chastity belt": Avoiding seduction in Tonga. In Kulick & Willson (1995:168-85).

Mott, Luiz. 1995. The gay movement and human rights in Brazil. In Murray (1995:221-30).

Murray, Stephen O. 1979. The art of gay insulting. *Anthropological Linguistics* 21:211-23.

—. 1980a. *Latino Homosexuality.* San Francisco: El Instituto Obregón.

—. 1980b. Lexical and institutional elaboration: the "species homosexual" in Guatemala. *Anthropological Linguistics* 22:177-86.

—. 1983. Fuzzy sets and "abominations." *Man* 18:396-99.

—. 1984a, *Social theory/homosexual realities.* New York: Gay Academic Union (=Gai Saber Monograph 3).

—. 1984b. Socially structuring prototype semantics. *Forum Linguisticum* 8:95-102.

—. 1987. *Male homosexuality in Central and South America.* New York: Gay Academic Union (=Gai Saber Monograph 5).

—. 1992. *Oceanic homosexualities.* New York: Garland.

—. 1995. *Latin American male homosexualities.* Albuquerque: University of New Mexico Press.

—. 1996a. *American gay.* Chicago: University of Chicago Press.

—. 1996b. Male homosexuality in Guatemala: Possible insights and certain confusions from sleeping with the natives. In Leap & Lewin (1996:236-60).

—. 1997. The will not to know: Islamic accommodations of male homosexuality. In Murray & Roscoe (1997:14-54).

—. 1998. *American sociolinguistics.* Amsterdam: John Benjamins.

—. 2000. *Homosexualities.* Chicago: University of Chicago Press.

—. 2002. Gender-mixing roles, gender-crossing roles, and the sexuality of transgendered roles. *Reviews in Anthropology.* In press.

Murray, Stephen O., and Manuel Arboleda G. 1995 [1982]. Stigma transformation and relexification: *Gay* in Latin America. In Murray (1995:138-44.)

Murray, Stephen O., and Wayne R. Dynes. 1995. Hispanic homosexuals: A Spanish lexicon. In Murray (1995:180-92).

Murray, Stephen O., and Will Roscoe. *Islamic homosexualities.* New York: New York University Press.

—. 1998. *Boy-wives and female husbands: Studies of African homosexualities.* New York: St. Martin's Press.

NACLA Report on the Americas. 1998. Sexual politics in Latin America. *NACLA Report on the Americas* 31 (4):16-44.

Nachman, Steven R. 1984. "Lies my informants told me." *Journal of Anthropological Research* 40:536-55.

Narayan, Kirin. 1993. How native is a "native" anthropologist? *American Anthropologist* 95:671-86.

Nash, June, and María Patricia Fernández-Kelly. 1983. *Women, men, and the international division of labor*. Albany: State University of New York Press.

Nieto S., Elba María. 1989. *El delito de la violación sexual en Honduras: Causística judicial*. Tegucigalpa: Comité Hondureño de Mujeres por la Paz "Visitación Padilla."

Núñez Noriega, Guillermo. 1994. *Sexo entre varones: Poder y resistencia en el campo sexual*. Hermosillo, Mexico: El Colegio de Sonora.

Padilla, A. Leon. 1981. *El machismo en Honduras*. Tegucigalpa: UNAH.

Parker, Richard G. 1999. *Beneath the equator: Cultures of desire, male homosexuality, and emerging gay communities in Brazil*. New York: Routledge.

Pastor Fasquelle, Rodolfo. 1975. *Desarrollo urbano en la Honduras colonial*. New Orleans, LA.

—. 1990. *Biografía de San Pedro Sula: 1536-1954*. San Pedro Sula: Centro Editorial.

Ponce, Alonso. 1873. Relación breve y verdadera de algunas cosas de las muchas que le sucedieron al padre fray Alonso Ponce en las provincias de la Nueva España, siendo comisario general de aquellas partes...escrita por dos religiosos, sus compañeros," 2 vols. Madrid: mpr. de la Viuda de Calero.

Prieur, Annick. 1998. *Mema's house, Mexico City: On transvestites, queens, and machos*. Chicago: University of Chicago Press.

Ramírez, Rafael L. 1993, 1999. *What it means to be a man: Reflections on Puerto Rican masculinity*. New Brunswick, NJ: Rutgers University Press.

Relación hecha a Su Majestad por Alonso Contreras Guevara Gobernador de Honduras, *BAGG* XI (1946):5-19.

Rich, Adrienne. 1980. Compulsory heterosexuality and lesbian existence. *Signs* 5:631-60.

Romney, A. Kimball, Susan C. Weller, and William H. Batchelder. 1986. Culture as consensus: A theory of culture and informant accuracy. *American Anthropologist* 88:313-38.

Rubin, Gayle. 1975. The traffic in women: Notes on the "political economy" of sex. In *Towards an anthropology of women*, ed. by Rayna Reiter. New York: Monthly Review Press, pp. 157-210.

——. 1984. Thinking sex: Notes for a radical theory of the politics of sexuality. In *Pleasure and danger: Exploring female sexuality*, ed. by Carole Vance. London: Routledge & Kegan Paul, pp. 267-319.

Salomón, Leticia. 1993. *La violencia en Honduras, 1980-1993*. Tegucigalpa: Centro de Documentación de Honduras (CEDOH); Comisionado Nacional para la Protección de los Derechos Humanos.

Schifter, Jacobo. 1989. *La formación de una contracultura: Homosexualismo y SIDA en Costa Rica*. San José: Guayacán.

——. 1998. *Lila's house: Male prostitution in Latin America*. New York: Haworth.

—. 1999. *From toads to queens: Transvestism in a Latin American setting.* New York: Haworth.

—. 2000. *Public Sex in a Latin Society.* New York: Haworth.

Schifter, Jacobo, and Peter Aggleton. 1999. *Cacherismo* in a San José brothel—aspects of male sex work in Costa Rica. In Aggleton (1999:141-58).

Schifter, Jacobo, and Johnny Madrigal Pana. 1992. *Hombres que aman hombres.* San José: Ediciones Ilep-SIDA.

Sears, James T., and Walter L. Williams, eds. 1997. *Overcoming heterosexism and homophobia: Strategies that work.* New York: Columbia University Press.

Sedgwick, Eve Kosofsky. 1990. *Epistemology of the closet.* Berkeley: University of California Press.

Stephen, Lynn. 1989. Anthropology and the politics of facts, knowledge, and history. *Dialectical Anthropology* 14:259-69.

Stevens, Evelyn P. 1973. *Marianismo*: The other face of *machismo* in Latin America. In *Female and Male in Latin America*, ed. by Anne Pescatello. Pittsburgh: University of Pittsburgh Press.

Stone, Doris. 1954. *Estampas de Honduras.* México, D.F.: Impresora Galve.

Taylor, Clark L. 1978. *El ambiente.* Ph.D. dissertation, University of California.

—1985. Mexican male homosexual interaction in public contexts. *Journal of Homosexuality* 11 (3/4):117-36.

Taylor, William B. 1987. The Virgin of Guadalupe in New Spain: an inquiry into the social history of Marian devotion. *American ethnologist* 14:9-33.

Turner, Ralph. 1978. The role and the self. *American Journal of Sociology* 84:1-23.

UIES. 1993. *San Pedro Sula: Población y desarrollo en los 90's*. San Pedro Sula: UIES.

VanMaanen, Joseph. 1988. *Tales of the Field*. Chicago: University of Chicago Press.

Vigil, James Diego, and Steve C. Yun. 1996. Southern California gangs: Comparative ethnicity and social control. In *Gangs in America*, ed. by C. Ronald Huff (2nd edition). Thousand Oaks, CA,: Sage, pp. 139-56.

Ward, Thomas W. Lecture of January 28, 1998 in course "Cross-Cultural Research on Urban Gangs" (Anth 371m) at the University of Southern California, Anthropology Department.

Warren, Carol A. B. 1977. Fieldwork in the gay world. *Journal of Social Issues* 33:93-107.

Wax, Murray L. 1980. Paradoxes of "consent" in the practice of fieldwork. *Social Problems* 27:272-83.

Weber, Max. 1958[1904-05]. *The Protestant ethic and the spirit of capitalism*. New York: Scribner's.

—. 1978[1920]. *Economy and Society*. Berkeley: University of California Press.

Whitam, Frederick L. 1992. *Bayot* and callboy: Homosexual-heterosexual relations in the Philippines. In Murray (1992:231-48).

Whitam, Frederick L., and Robin M. Mathy. 1986. *Male homosexuality in four societies: Brazil, Guatemala, the Philippines, and the United States.* New York: Praeger.

White, C. Todd. 1998. The camp. In *Fools and jesters in literature, art, and history: A bio-bibliographic sourcebook,* ed. by Vicki Janik. Westport, CT: Greenwood Press, pp. 113-19.

Wikan, Unni. 1984. Shame and honour: a contestable pair. *Man* (n.s.) 19:635-52.

Williams, Walter L. 1986. *The spirit and the flesh: Sexual diversity in American Indian culture.* Boston: Beacon Press.

—. 1993 Being gay and doing research on homosexuality in non-Western cultures. *Journal of Sex Research* 30:115-20.

Wolf, Eric R. 1999. *Envisioning Power.* Berkeley: University of California Press.

Zapata, Luis. 1985[1979]. *El vampiro de la Colonia Roma: Las aventuras, desventuras y sueños de Adonis García.* México, D.F.: Grijalbo.

0-595-22681-7